fanny zedenius

macramé

the craft of creative
knotting for your home

photography by kim lightbody

quadrille

contents

introduction

In Swedish, the word *pyssel* is used to describe all sorts of crafting and creative activity – be it drawing, painting, scrapbooking, sewing, crocheting, pottery or beading. For as long as I can remember, I have been addicted to *pyssel*. As a child I would always wait for class to be over so I could continue with my current project – although I usually couldn't wait, which was why all of my school books were filled with drawings. In upper secondary school I sewed my own clothes (yes, I did look quite ridiculous at times) and in high school I brought my knitting so I would be able to concentrate better during class. When I was stressing over exams and grades it was always my *pyssel* projects that would take my mind off problems, make me wind down and help me to see things clearly again.

Fanny Zedenius

People would often ask if I was going to pursue my creative interests and make them into something more than a hobby. But I had other plans, plus I could never stick to one kind of crafting long enough to take it further anyway. In 2014 I started an Instagram account called Createaholic and stumbled upon macramé. I fell head over heels in love with the craft and taught myself the crucial knots, using whatever string I had at home. This craft was different to all the others I had explored and moved on from – macramé was addictive in a whole new way.

So what is it about macramé that makes it so special? Personally, I love the fact that it hardly requires any tools other than your hands, and – while you can learn many techniques and knots – you can create incredible pieces using only one kind of knot. More importantly, no matter how many wall hangings, plant hangers or dream catchers I have made, I never seem to run out of ideas for new designs. There are an infinite number of ways you can combine different knots. It is amazing what you are able to create by simply knotting cords together.

I also find macramé to be the most meditative craft I have explored. You can let your mind wander while your hands do the knotting and there is little need for counting and keeping track of your work as in crochet or knitting. I would come home from eight hours of office work, just to work another six hours on my on-going project. And I can honestly say that I have never been less stressed in my whole life.

The generation before mine remembers macramé from the 1970s, and they either feel very nostalgic about it, or wish it had never come back in style. What we are seeing now, however, is a modern take on macramé that has become wildly popular for home décor. Suddenly, macramé is everywhere! While the trend continues to grow, the thirst for learning the craft becomes more apparent. This book is my way of reaching out to anyone wanting to learn macramé; it teaches you both the basics and introduces you to some of the more advanced techniques and a variety of possibilities. I hope you will have as much fun with your knotting as I had putting together this book for you!

Fanny's plant hangers soaking up the sun in her Stockholm apartment

basics

how to use this book

Whether you are a beginner or have previous experience with macramé, you will find this book an excellent tool to help you start knotting your own macramé projects. If you are a beginner, I recommend reading through Macramé Secrets first and then trying out one of the easier plant hanger or wall hanging projects in the project section, found at the beginning of their respective sections. While working on a project, refer back to the knots section for instructions. If you already have knotting experience, you may want to try out some of the more advanced projects found later on in each section, or try knotting some basic patterns from the pattern section to design your own projects.

macramé secrets (page 8)
This section begins by going through the different materials you can choose to work with and the different tools and equipment that make the knotting easier. You will also find advice on how to tackle common problems that us knotters face in the beginning.

knots (page 17)
The gallery provides step-by-step instructions and illustrations for 34 different knots, including guidelines for how much cord each knot requires. Once you have mastered the most commonly used knots, you will find this chapter helpful when experimenting on your own with new designs and knots.

patterns (page 29)
The patterns section gives you seven examples of how to combine knots to create patterns that you can include in wall hangings or other projects. Each pattern has step-by-step instructions and illustrations. Dimensions are not provided here, since the patterns can be made to any scale and are meant as inspiration for your own designs.

projects (page 41)
This section offers a selection of 21 projects divided into four different categories: plant hangers, wall hangings, dream catchers and finally a variety of other macramé projects. The latter will give you some ideas about more ways to create or decorate almost anything with macramé!

The projects all have step-by-step instructions and annotated illustrations. You might find that you prefer to just follow the illustrations, or that you want to read all instructions thoroughly. The illustrations vary in style depending on the scale of the project and the level of detail needed. The larger wall hangings, and some of the other projects, have charts illustrating the completed project where only the knots are highlighted and the linking cords are left blank. Keep track of the number of knots in the chart to follow along.

The projects specify which cord to use and the dimensions are given in both centimetres and inches. The cords are referred to by their position, with cord number 1 always starting from the left. After each step is completed, the cords are renumbered so that cord number 1 is always the first cord on the left. You can experiment with other materials if you wish, but it is important to remember that the specified dimensions are given with the stated cord in mind, and should you use a thinner or thicker cord the dimensions will not be the same. Thicker rope requires longer lengths. The dimensions will also be affected by how tightly you tie the knots. If you know you tend to tie loose knots, you might need to allow extra length for all your cords. In general, always work with more cord than you think you need!

macramé
secrets

One of the reasons I love macramé is that it
is quite easy to learn, but at the same time you
can always keep exploring this craft and evolving
your style. As a beginner you might feel a bit
insecure, and there is a lot of trial and error to
go through before you will feel really confident
in your knotting. Here are some of my secrets
to successful knotting to give you a boost!

materials

Choosing the right material is an essential part of macramé, because the design can look very different depending on what elements you use. Try different materials to find your personal style.

Cord

Basically any type of cord can be used in macramé, but the most common are cotton, hemp, jute, T-shirt yarn or polyester. Out of these, most macramé artists work with cotton. While any strand material can be used for macramé, consider whether you plan on having your project outside or if it runs the risk of getting wet in any way. If so, you might want to choose a material that fits the purpose.

Another aspect to consider is whether to choose a braided or twined cord. Braided cords are less prone to fraying, while twined cord is much easier to fray. Finally, consider the cord thickness; with thicker cord you will be able to create impressive, large-scale pieces, and with finer cord you can achieve a stunning intricacy in your patterns.

Rings

Rings are often used when making plant hangers. You can use any material, as long as the ring will be able to carry the weight of the plant. Personally I prefer wooden or metal rings.

Beads

You can use absolutely any type of bead or charm in your macramé, be it in a plant hanger, wall hanging, curtain or a lantern. This is where you can be a little extra creative!

Branches or dowels

For wall hangings, you will need to find a good dowel or branch as a support. A 'dowel' can be of any material – for example you could use a copper pipe for a stunning effect.

Hoops

Metal and wooden hoops can be used in various ways to make creative projects. They are often used to make dream catchers and lanterns or mobiles. Wooden rings can be harder to find, but they look beautiful through the cords.

tools & equipment

Some tools are essential in macramé, while others just make the knotting much easier. Here are some suggestions for your macramé toolbox.

Measuring tape
You'll need this to measure out the lengths of your cords.

Scissors
Obviously one of the most essential tools, to cut the cord!

Tape
Use tape on the ends of your cords to keep them from fraying. I prefer masking tape since it will not leave any marks on the cord.

S-hooks
You can't have too many S-hooks! Use them when you hang your work in progress.

Clothes rack
A clothes rack is just what you need in order to work comfortably. Any type of clothes rack will do, although one that is adjustable in height can be extra helpful. Of course, something similar to a clothes rack can also work – for instance, working from your curtain rail.

Crochet hook
A crochet hook can be helpful when threading beads on to rope, or to pull a cord through a space between or within a knot.

Pliers
I use pin-nose pliers when I need to adjust my knots. For example, I sometimes find I have tied a knot too loosely, so I use pliers to tighten the knot and adjust the adjacent knots if necessary.

how to find rope

This is by far the most frustrating part for an aspiring knotter, because good rope can be quite hard to find; where to find it is the most common question macramé artists are asked.

To get you started, check out your local craft shop or hobby specialist. They will almost certainly have some good quality cords, and will probably have a selection of different materials.

If you plan on becoming a little more serious with your knotting, however, and want to try the large-scale projects, you will need large volumes of rope – and this is where you might want to find more affordable suppliers. Search for suppliers who specialize specifically in selling rope – they usually concentrate on rope for nautical purposes, but they may also have a part of their business that deals in hobby rope or rope for crafting.

Another way to find good rope is to go straight to the source – a rope factory in your country. Unfortunately such factories sometimes only sell in bulk to other suppliers and not directly to individuals – but if so, you can do some detective work to find out who these suppliers are.

If you search for rope online, use these keywords: rope, cord; specific rope/cord thickness – 2.5mm ($1/8$in)/4mm ($3/16$in)/6mm ($1/4$in); twined/braided/sash cord; specific materials – cotton/hemp/jute.

how to tackle large wall hangings

Large wall hangings are not necessarily harder to make, they usually just involve a lot more knots and time. But here are a few notes to help answer some of the questions you might have, or tackle the problems you might face during the work process.

What kind of dowel or branch should I use?

It probably goes without saying, but large-scale macramé can be very heavy. One of the worst things that can happen after finishing a large wall hanging is that your supporting rod breaks. So be very picky when you choose your dowel or branch and make sure it will be able to carry the weight.

How do I know how much rope I need?

As for all macramé projects, this really depends on what kind of design you are planning for your wall hanging, and on the thickness of your rope. For example, if you plan on making a 100 x 100cm (39 3/8 x 39 3/8 in) wall hanging, think about the following before you cut:

Will I be using knots all over the whole area or will I have large parts without any knots?

If you are using knots all over the panel, your cords will probably have to be around five times the length of the finished piece (perhaps even more if you are making a really intricate pattern). So in other words, each cord would have to be 5m (5 1/2 yd) – but as they are folded in half before being attached to the branch/dowel, you would need to cut them at 10m (11yd) long. If, however, you are using a much less intricate pattern with the knots further apart and parts without knots, you might only need the cords to be double the length of the finished piece.

Will there be more knots in parts of your wall hanging?

For example, you might want to have more knots in the middle of the wall hanging, in which case your cords in the middle will need to be longer than the ones on the sides.

Any advice for neat knotting with all the long cords?

When you work on large-scale wall hangings you inevitably work with a lot of long cords. You might find it easier to bundle each cord to prevent them from tangling together, by rolling them up and either tying a little knot around or using a rubber band. This can also help as you tie the knots, since it can take a lot of time just to pass the cords through if they are very long.

How to work with clove hitches in your wall hanging?

If you are planning on including clove hitches in your wall hanging, try to plan ahead where you want these to be. Clove hitches use up a lot of filler cord if you stretch a sequence of clove hitches across a large area. If you cut your filler cords and working cords the same length, your filler cords will end up much shorter than the rest of the cords – this is especially true for large-scale projects. So, for example, if your 100 x 100cm (39 3/8 x 39 3/8 in) wall hanging has one row of horizontal clove hitches across the whole width of the piece, then be sure to cut the filler cord with the extra 100cm (39 3/8 in) that it will need.

How thick should my rope be?

This is not rocket science: if your rope is 6mm (1/4 in) thick, you won't be able to include as many cords over the same area as you would if you used a 2.5mm (1/8 in) thick rope. Also, a thicker rope means fewer knots and vice versa.

What do I do if I find a mistake somewhere?

One of the things I love about macramé is that if you make a mistake, it isn't the end of the world. As long as you haven't cut any rope, you can always redo the knots. However, finding a mistake that you made in the beginning of a large-scale project can be very frustrating. I am sorry to say that the only way of fixing it is to untie the knots and then tie them again. Or you can always accept the little flaws that make your wall hanging unique!

fraying

Frayed cord – sometimes you want to avoid it and other times you wish you could fray faster. Having frayed ends or not gives a finished piece a very different look. While there is a very easy way to avoid fraying ends, there is no magical method to fray quickly; it does take a little time and patience but can be quite meditative.

What can I do to stop the rope from fraying?

The easiest thing is to choose a braided rope. Braided rope will hardly fray at all, while twined rope can fray by itself. If you are using twined rope but do not want your ends to fray, tape all the ends after you have cut them and remove the tape carefully once your piece is finished. To make sure fraying doesn't happen to finished pieces, you might want to tie knots at the ends of the cords – for example, an overhand knot (see page 18) or a barrel knot (see page 25).

How do I fray faster?

If you know you want frayed ends, choose twined rope for your project as it will be much easier to fray than braided rope. In either case, you have to either unbraid or untwine the rope to get frayed ends. For me, the easiest way of fraying is to roll the twined rope in the 'wrong' direction, making the twined parts separate. Once they are, comb the rope with your fingers until they stop tangling. Then use a hard brush to really separate all the fibres.

dip dyeing

To dip dye or not to dip dye? This decision is always a little delicate. On the one hand, the finished piece looks stunning the way it is; on the other, it might look even more striking with added colour. If you decide to go for it, choose to use chemical or natural dyes depending on your style. Even though your first try might not give the exact result you imagined – it will still look amazing!

be kind to your body!

It might sound silly, but for me this is a very important part of the knotting craft. Macramé can definitely be hard on your body, especially if you are knotting for long periods at a time.

Rope burns, blisters and shoulder pains are common amongst us knotters, and as much as I love this craft, I do sometimes have to take breaks to let my body rest and recover.

So what can you do to be as kind to your body as possible when you are delving into macramé?

Here is what I do

Use first aid plasters or even gloves to protect your fingers when knotting.

To avoid having to bend your back or stand in an uncomfortable position, raise or lower your work as required as you proceed.

Regularly switch between sitting and standing.

Take pauses and do some simple stretching.

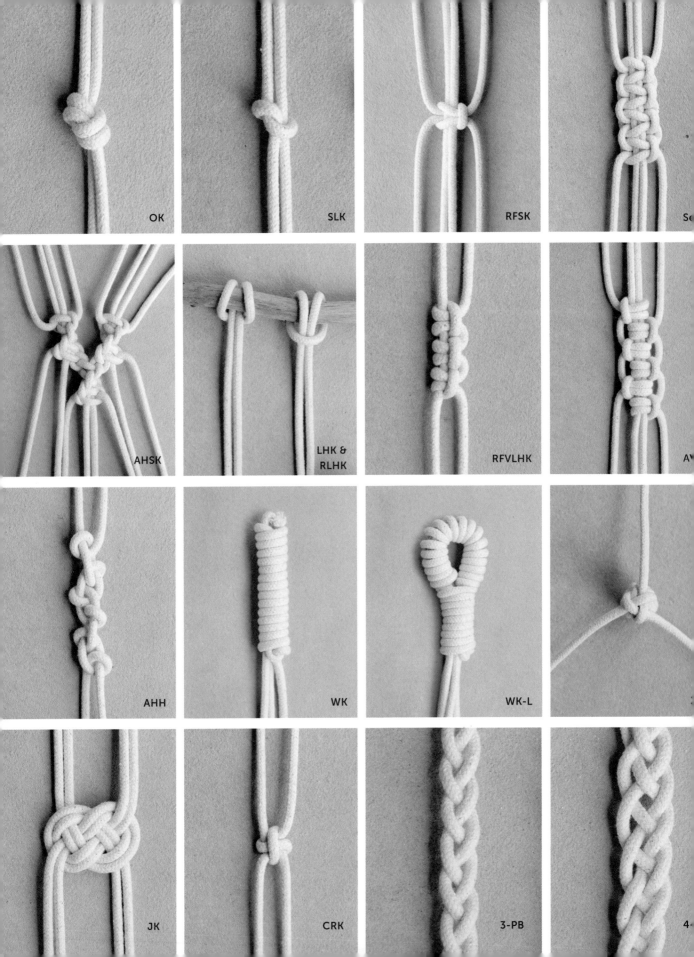

OK

SLK

RFSK

Se

AHSK

LHK &
RLHK

RFVLHK

A

AHH

WK

WK-L

JK

CRK

3-PB

4

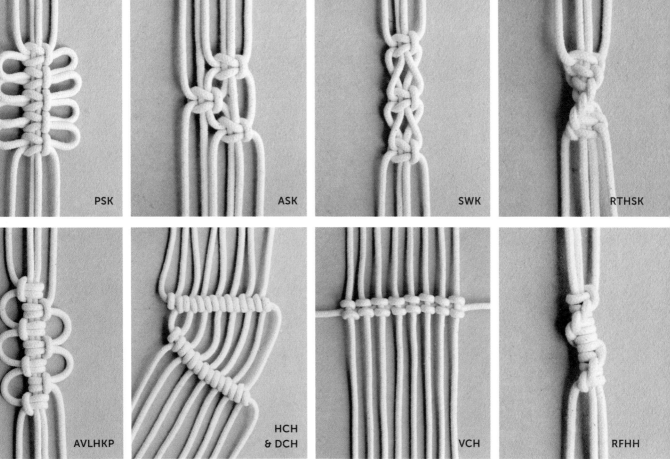

PSK

ASK

SWK

RTHSK

AVLHKP

HCH
& DCH

VCH

RFHH

4-CK

BK

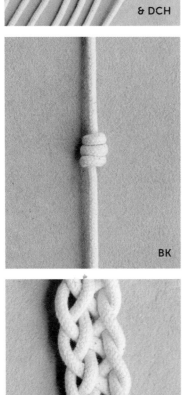

knots

This knot gallery will take you through a total of 34 different knots. At the heart of macramé are just a handful of simple knots – learn the basic square knot, clove hitch and lark's head knot and you will be good to go. Add in the half square knot, half hitch, Josephine knot and crown knot and you will be able to make marvellous creations. I promise that the knots in this book are all you will ever need to know in order to become an expert at macramé.

5-PB

6-PB

bundling knots

Knotting can sometimes become overwhelming due to a large number of cords. Bundling cords together keeps them organized during your knotting, and secures the ends.

Overhand knot OK

The overhand knot is an easy way of bundling together any number of cords.

Step 1 Hold the cords together and fold them into a loop. Pass the ends of the cords through the loop.

Step 2 Pull the ends firmly to tighten the knot.

Step 3 The overhand knot is finished. Don't pull the knot too tight, as you will want to undo it again when you need to work with the cords.

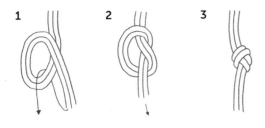

Slipknot SLK

The slipknot, also known as a gathering knot, is a small and simple knot that can gather any number of cords together.

Step 1 Take one of the cords and use it as the working cord. Wrap it around the other cord(s), and pass the end of the working cord down through the loop it has formed.

Step 2 Tighten the knot by pulling the working cord firmly.

Step 3 The slipknot is finished. Again, don't tie it too tight as you'll need to release it later.

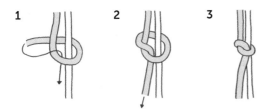

square knots

Square knots (SK) are commonly created using two filler cords in the centre, with a working cord on each side. The knots can face left or right, depending on the sequence in which they are tied. This is one of the most common macramé knots, used in most macramé patterns. By alternating filler and working cords on rows of square knots, you are able to create a net-like pattern.

Length of cord per knot Takes 4–6 times the length of the finished knot or sennit.

Right-facing square knot RFSK

A right-facing knot (RFSK) has a vertical bump on the knot that appears to the right. A left-facing knot (LFSK) is tied the same way as a right-facing but mirrored. Follow the instructions for a right-facing, but replace cord A with B, left with right and vice versa.

Step 1 Move cord B to the left across the white filler cords, forming a loop, and behind cord A.

Step 2 Move cord A behind the filler cords, and pass it up through the loop from behind. Pull cord A gently to the right, and B gently to the left, while holding the filler cords straight.

Step 3 Move cord B to the right across the filler cords, forming a loop, and behind cord A. Move cord A behind the filler cords, and pass it up through the loop created by cord B, from behind.

Step 4 Tighten the knot by pulling cords A and B while holding the filler cords straight.

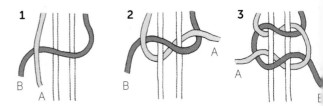

Square knots sennit SK Sennit

Tying the square knot into sennits is a technique that is often used in plant hangers, or when making macramé bracelets, for example. You can use any number of filler cords, but the most usual method is with two – as in these illustrations.

Step 1 Begin the sennit by tying either a right-facing square knot or a left-facing square knot (see above).

Step 2 A sennit takes form when you tie a series of matching square knots placed directly underneath each other. If you began with a right-facing square knot, continue by tying a new right-facing square knot placed directly underneath the previous one. The same goes for the left-facing square knot; simply repeat the knot again to create a sennit.

Step 3 Tighten the knot by pulling the working cords, while holding the filler cords straight.

TIP To know which cord to continue with at any stage of the sennit, always begin with the cord coming out behind the vertical 'bump'. In this illustration the last bump is to the left, therefore you should use the left working cord next.

Step 4 Repeat steps 2–3 until your sennit is the length you require.

TIP One way of checking that you are tightening the cords equally firmly is to make sure that the 'front' and the 'back' of the sennit look exactly the same.

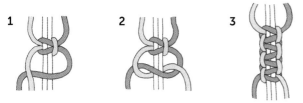

Alternating square knot ASK
Rows of square knots can be offset to create a net-like pattern.

Step 1 Tie a row of square knots. On the second row, use the outer working cord of each pair of adjacent square knots as the filler cords and the nearest pair of filler cords as the working cords, so that the second row of square knots will be offset.

Step 2 Tighten each knot, placing it close to the first row to create a fine net, or position it further apart from the first row to create a looser net.

Step 3 Continue alternating the filler and working cords used to tie the knots on every other row.

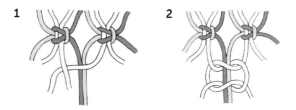

Picot square knot PSK
The picot design is made by creating decorative loops along both sides of a sennit of square knots.

Step 1 Tie a sennit of square knots leaving an equal amount of space between each knot. The larger the space, the bigger the loops of the picot design.

Step 2 Holding the filler cords straight with one hand, slide the knots upwards using the other. Leave a little space between the knots to form a chain of round loops.

Step 3 Or you can slide the knots close to each other to create a classic picot design.

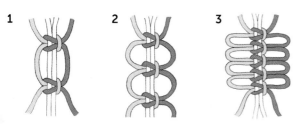

Switch knot SWK
This decorative pattern is made by switching the working cords and filler cords between each knot. This technique also means that all cords will be used up equally.

Step 1 After completing the first square knot, move the working cords over the filler cords and into the centre to become the filler cords for the second knot.

Step 2 The filler cords on the first square knot are now the working cords on the second knot.

Step 3 Continue in this way, switching the filler and working cords after completing each knot. Leave enough space between the knots to reveal the decorative pattern.

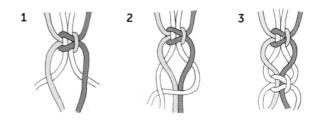

Right-twisting half square knot RTHSK

The half square knot, also known as a spiral knot, half knot spiral or spiral stitch, is commonly used in macramé patterns. The right-twisting half square knot is created by repeatedly tying only half of the right-facing square knot. To make a spiral with left-twisting half square knots (LTHSK), simply tie half of the left-facing square knot in repeat.

Step 1 Pass cord B to the left over the filler cords, forming a loop, and behind cord A. Move cord A behind the filler cords, and pass it up through the loop from behind. Pull cord A gently to the right, and B gently to the left, while holding the filler cords straight.

Step 2 Pass cord A to the left over the filler cords, forming a loop, and behind cord B. Move cord B behind the filler cords, and pass it up through the loop from behind. Make sure that you pull the working cords equally tight. The knot should look the same from the front and the back.

Step 3 As you repeat steps 1–2, the spiral forms. The knot is reversible, so when the knot has twisted half a turn, just continue from the "back" as before. If necessary, push the knots upwards while holding the filler cords straight.

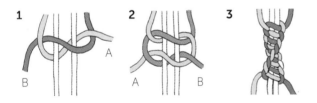

Alternating half square knot AHSK

This is another way of creating a net as you alternate the working and filler cords. When using this knot, you will need to tie the amount of half square knots it takes for the spiral to turn.

Step 1 Tie a row of spirals using half square knots and make sure the spirals complete at least one turn.

For the second row, alternate the working cords and filler cords and tie a new row of spirals.

Step 2 Make sure the spirals complete at least one turn, and then continue with as many new rows as you wish.

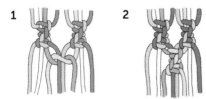

lark's head knot

Lark's head knots are the most common way of attaching your cords to a dowel or an anchor cord. The best technique adds a loose folded cord to the filler cord, but if one of the ends is already attached somewhere else, just tie the knot using the second technique.

Length of cord per knot

Takes 6–7 times the length of the finished knot, but this also depends on the thickness of the filler cord or dowel.

Lark's head knot LHK

The lark's head knot is most commonly used to attach cords to a dowel or an anchor cord – for example when starting a wall hanging. The original knot has a horizontal bump facing you.

Step 1 Fold the cord in half and then fold the loop away from you over the dowel or anchor cord.

Step 2 Pass the 2 cord ends through the loop at the front and pull the cords to tighten the knot

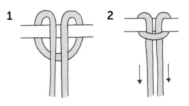

TIP These illustrations show an alternative way of tying the lark's head knot. This is a useful method when you wish to attach a cord where one of the ends is already attached somewhere (see the Atlantis wall hanging on page 75).

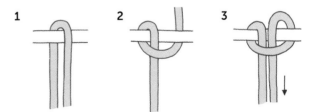

Reverse lark's head knot RLHK

The reverse lark's head knot, most commonly used to attach cords to a dowel or an anchor cord, is worked in the same way as the standard version, but from the reverse so the bump is hidden.

Step 1 Fold the cord in half and then fold the loop towards you over the dowel or anchor cord.

Step 2 Pass the 2 cord ends through the loop at the back and pull the cords to tighten the knot.

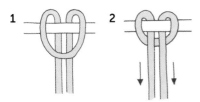

TIP This version can also be tied in the alternative way if one end is already attached somewhere.

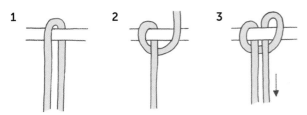

Right-facing vertical lark's head knot RFVLHK

This technique allows you to tie a sennit using only two cords – although you can, of course, use any number of filler cords. To make a sennit of left-facing vertical lark's head knots, simply use the same technique but mirrored, wrapping the working cord in step 1 from the left over the filler cord.

Step 1 Take the right working cord and pass it over the left filler cord, then pass it around behind and bring it forward through the loop from back to front.

Step 2 Pass the working cord around behind the filler cord again, then take it backward through the loop from front to back.

Step 3 Finish the knot by pulling the working cord to tighten it, while holding the filler cord straight. Repeat steps 1–3 to create a sennit of the required length.

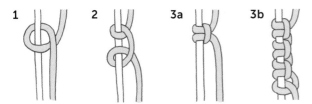

Alternating vertical lark's head knot AVLHK

You can also alternate left- and right-facing vertical lark's head knots, which will create a broader sennit than, for example, a sennit of square knots. Here, these are tied over 2 filler cords – so a total of 4 cords – but you can also tie them using just 1 filler cord.

Step 1 You can begin with either a left-facing or right-facing vertical lark's head knot; here the left-hand cord is used to tie a left-facing vertical lark's head knot over the 2 filler cords.

Step 2 Alternate the working cord, so now the right-hand cord is used to tie a right-facing vertical lark's head knot over the 2 filler cords.

Step 3 Continue the sennit by alternating left- and right-facing vertical lark's head knots. The knots should be placed as close together as possible, keeping the links between knots on both sides straight and even.

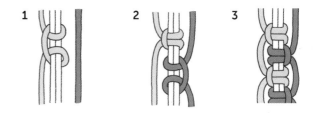

Alternating vertical lark's head knots with picots
AVLHKP

Another way of making a sennit with alternating vertical lark's head knots is to make picots on the linking cords between the knots.

Step 1 Begin a regular sennit of alternating vertical lark's head knots by tying one left-facing and one right-facing vertical lark's head knot. Leave a gap between each knot then push them all up towards the previous knot. The bigger the gap, the bigger the loop of the picot.

Step 2 Continue alternating left- and right-facing vertical lark's head knots, spacing the knots at an equal distance and pushing them up, until you have a sennit of the required length.

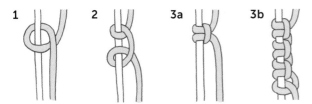

clove hitch knots

Apart from the square knot, the clove hitch is the most commonly used knot in wall hangings. Since it can be tied horizontally, diagonally or vertically, it is easy to use when you wish to make more intricate patterns, such as butterflies or leaves. Each knot is made with two loops around a filler cord. For horizontal and diagonal clove hitches, make sure your filler cord is long enough to create the desired length of lines.

Length of cord per knot

Takes 5–7 times the length of one finished knot (for the working cord).

Horizontal clove hitch HCH

The horizontal clove hitch forms a straight line across a panel, with the filler cord running through it going either left-to-right or right-to-left, or bending back and forth.

Step 1 To make a line going left-to-right, use the furthest left cord as filler cord, holding it horizontally in front of all the other cords on the panel. Use the next cord to the right as the working cord for the first clove hitch, first bringing it forward, up and around the filler cord towards the left. Pull the working cord to tighten the loop while tilting the filler cord slightly upwards.

Step 2 Finish the first clove hitch by taking the working cord around the filler cord again to the right of the first wrap, passing the end though the loop formed under the filler cord. Pull the working cord to tighten the knot. Repeat steps 1–2 for each cord to the right in turn.

Step 3 To make another line underneath the first, bend the filler cord in front of the other cords on the panel horizontally from right-to-left. Repeat steps 1–2, but beginning with the right-hand cord and working each knot in reverse towards the left.

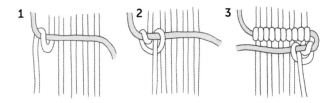

Diagonal clove hitch DCH

The diagonal clove hitch uses the same technique as the horizontal clove hitch, but refers to a line of tilted clove hitches.

Step 1 To knot a diagonal line left-to-right, use the furthest left cord as filler cord, holding it diagonally in front of the other cords on the panel. Use the next cord to the right as the working cord for the first clove hitch, then continue working to the right, placing each clove hitch slightly below the previous one to make a diagonal line of knots.

Step 2 To make another diagonal underneath the first, bend the filler cord and hold it in front of all the other cords diagonally right-to-left. Repeat step 1, but beginning with the right-hand cord and working each knot in reverse towards the left.

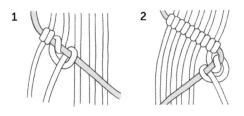

Vertical clove hitch VCH

Vertical clove hitches differ from the horizontal and diagonal versions in that the vertical cords are used as filler cords, while the working cord is the same across the panel. The individual clove hitch is still tied the same way, only tilted 90 degrees.

Step 1 To make a line going left-to-right, use the cord on the left-hand side as the first filler cord. Wrap the working cord around the filler cord as shown, then tighten the loop by gently pulling the working cord.

Step 2 Finish the first clove hitch by wrapping the working cord around the filler cord underneath the first wrap, passing the end though the loop. Pull on the working cord to tighten the knot.

Step 3 Repeat steps 1–2 to make a line of vertical knots.

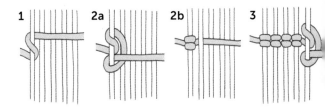

half hitch spiral

The half hitch spiral is the easiest way of creating a spiral. It is made by repeatedly wrapping the working cord around one or more filler cords.

Length of cord per knot
Takes 4–5 times the length of one finished spiral.

Right-facing half hitch RFHH
The working cord is placed to the right of the filler cords and wraps around them from the right, forming a spiral that twists from right to left. To make a left-twisting half hitch spiral, simply use the same technique but mirrored, wrapping the working cord in step 1 from left over the filler cords to the right.

Step 1 Pass the working cord over in front of the filler cords and wrap it around them, passing it up through the loop.

Step 2 Pull the working cord gently to tighten the first right-facing half hitch, while holding the filler cords straight.

Step 3 Repeat steps 1–2 and then push the knots upwards so they are close together.

Step 4 Continue to repeat steps 1–3 until you have the desired length of spiral.

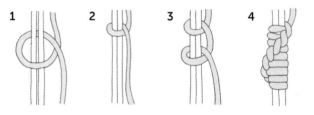

Alternating half hitch AHH
This technique is an easy way of making a sennit using only two cords. The alternating half hitch alternates the working cord and filler cord for each half hitch.

Step 1 Begin by tying either a left-facing half hitch knot (as shown in the illustration) or a right-facing half hitch knot.

Step 2 Alternate your working cord and filler cord for the second half hitch.

Step 3 Repeat steps 1-2 to make a chain of alternating half hitches.

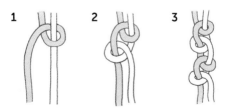

wrap knots

The wrap knot is perfect for gathering all your cords together in a neat way and can also be used to create loops. You will see it is commonly used in plant hanger designs. The wrap knot forms as you first create a loop with your working cord, wrap the cord around the loop and the filler cords, and finally secure it by passing it through the loop.

Length of cord per knot
Takes 8–10 times the length of the finished knot, but this depends on how many filler cords you have to wrap.

Wrap knot WK
The regular wrap knot is simply one working cord wrapped around any number of filler cords. The length of your working cord will depend on how long you want your wrap knot, how many filler cords you have, and the thickness of your cords. A good bit of advice is to take more cord than you think you will need! And practice makes perfect.

Step 1 Gather the filler cords together and place the working cord on top folded in a U-shape. Begin wrapping one end of the working cord around all the cords, starting at the top. For the first lap, hold the working cord in place with one hand (where the working cord passes over itself), while wrapping with the other hand. As you continue you can let go and turn the bundle around as you wrap, so you can make sure that all the laps are placed neatly together.

Step 2 Stop wrapping when you can see about a 1cm ($^3/_8$ in) of the folded loop left. Pass the working cord through the loop from the front.

Step 3 Pull the top of the working cord so that the loop slides up behind the wrapping. If you wish, you can now cut both the top and bottom ends of the working cord.

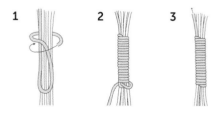

Wrap knot under a ring WK-R

The wrap knot is sometimes placed directly underneath something – either other knots, or perhaps a ring. Since it can be difficult to grasp how to tie the wrap knot this way, these instructions show how to tie a wrap knot under a ring. The finishing steps of the knot can be made in two ways – you might find that one works better for you than the other.

Step 1 Pass all cords through the ring, making sure your working cord for the wrap knot is extra-long. Fold the working cord in a U-shape. The length of the wrap knot will be from the ring to the bottom of the U, so make sure the U is the right length.

For the first lap, it might be easiest to hold the working cord in place with one hand (where the working cord passes over itself), while wrapping with the other hand. As you continue you can let go and turn the bundle around as you wrap, so you can make sure all the laps are placed neatly together.

Step 2 Stop wrapping when you can see about 1cm ($^3/_8$ in) of the folded loop left.

First

Step 2a Pass the working cord through the loop from the front.

Step 2b Use pliers to pull the top of the working cord so that the loop slides up behind the wrapping. As you pull, note which of the filler cords coming out of the wrap knot pulls up at the same time, and pull down on this to tighten the cord to the ring again.

Second

Step 3a Wrap a couple of loose laps around the wrap knot. Don't worry if it looks messy, you will correct this later. Pass the end of the working cord through the loop from the front.

Now find the place on the wrap knot where you left off before wrapping the loose laps, and simply continue to place the laps in the right order, keeping them tight.

Step 3b Pull the end of the working cord to tighten the last lap.

Wrap knot loop using only cord WK-L

The technique of creating a loop using the wrap knot can come in handy when making a plant hanger if you don't have a ring available. It is fairly easy – the loop is just made with two wrap knots, which means the working cord needs to be extra-long to allow enough to tie the second wrap knot.

Step 1 Begin by making a regular wrap knot. If you want the filler cords to be the same length at each end, the wrap knot needs to be placed in the middle of all the cords. Place the top end of the working cord together with the filler cords. Make the U-shape in the middle of the cords and make a regular wrap knot.

Step 2 Now bend the wrap knot around into a ring, pushing its ends together. Take the longer end of the working cord and make a second wrap knot around all of the other cords.

Step 3 Since you cannot pull the cord end to make the loop disappear behind the wrapping, as in the regular wrap knot, use finishing technique 3a as for the wrap knot placed under a ring on (see above). In other words stop wrapping when you can see about a 1cm ($^3/_8$ in) of the loop left, and wrap a couple of loose laps on top of the wrap knot before you pass the cord through the loop. Finish the wrap knot by going around tightening the laps, and finally pulling the working cord to tighten the last lap.

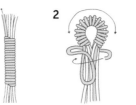

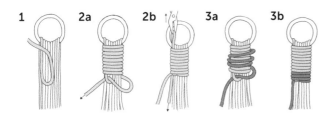

crown knots

The crown knot can sometimes feel a bit complicated, but the trick is just to get it started – it is much easier after the third sequence! The knot can be tied with three or more strands and, as you can see from the descriptions, the technique is the same for both three and four strands – placing each cord over the adjacent cord, tightening, and repeating. In some of the plant hanger projects the crown knot is made with four cords representing one strand, but the technique will be the same.

Length of cord per knot

Takes 4–5 times the length of the finished piece.

3-ply crown knot 3-CK

Using three strands for the crown knot forms a diagonally patterned 'tube'. Tie the knot from above, and 'build' with each sequence. To make the knot easier you may want to lay the cords on a table, so that they can be placed the right way without falling out of place.

Step 1 Begin by laying out your 3 strands in 3 different directions. You might have a knot that holds them together in the centre; otherwise hold them together with your non-dominant hand, using the other to tie the knot.

Step 2 Take any of the strands and fold it round over the strand next to it, creating a loop.

Step 3 Then take the second strand and fold it around over both the first strand and the third strand.

Step 4 Fold the third strand over both the second strand and the first strand, and pass it through the loop formed by the first strand. Gently pull each strand, one at a time, to tighten the knot.

Step 5 The first sequence is completed. Repeat steps 2–4 until your crown knot is the desired length.

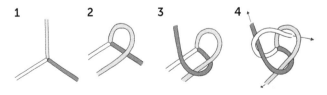

4-ply crown knot 4-CK

The crown knot is most commonly made with four strands, and four is the ultimate number to create the neatest knot.

Step 1 Lay out your 4 strands in 4 different directions. You can use a knot to hold them together in the centre; otherwise hold them with your non-dominant hand, using the other to tie the knot. If you use 2 strands, lay them across each other to form a cross.

Step 2 Take any of the strands and fold it round over the strand next to it, creating a loop. Then take the second strand and fold it around over both the first and the third strand.

Step 3 Take the third strand and fold it around over both the second and the fourth strand. For the fourth strand, fold it over the third then the first strand, and pass it through the loop formed by the first strand. Gently pull each strand, one at a time, to tighten the knot.

Step 4 The first sequence is completed. Repeat steps 2–3 until your crown knot is the desired length.

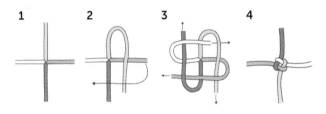

decorative knots

Barrel knot BK

The barrel knot, sometimes referred to as the coil knot, it is a very neat knot, created with one cord tied onto itself. If you wrap the cord three times, the knot will look almost like a bead and is therefore very decorative. The barrel knot can also be used to stop your cords from fraying, while looking really pretty. This knot takes 6–8 times the length of the finished knot.

Step 1 Bend the cord around to form a loop and wrap the end of the cord around the left side of the loop at least 3 times – more if you want a longer knot. To tighten the knot, hold the bottom end of the cord with one hand, while gently pulling the upper end of the cord upwards with your other hand.

Step 2 Secure the knot by pulling gently pulling on both ends.

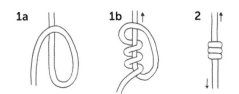

Josephine knot JK

The Josephine knot is a very decorative knot that can be tied with two or more cords. It looks difficult, and therefore quite impressive, but once you know how, it isn't difficult at all. This knot takes 2–3 times the height of the finished knot for each cord.

Step 1 Bend the cord A to form a loop and place cord B over the top of the loop. Form a second loop with cord B by weaving it round under the lower end of cord A, then over, under, over, and under again.

Step 2 You'll now have 2 interlocked loops. You can finish the knot by gently pulling cord A and B to tighten it.

If you would like to add 2 more cords to make a bigger Josephine knot, do not tighten the knot yet. Place cord C to the left, and cord D to the right.

Step 3 Simply pass cord C alongside cord A, and cord D alongside cord B and adjust if necessary so the cords lie flat beside each other. Finish the knot by gently pulling cords CA and BD.

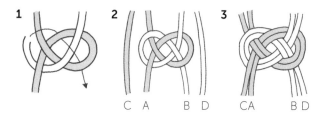

Cross knot CRK

The cross knot is a neat little knot, tied with two cords in the shape of a single cross or plus-mark.

Step 1 Begin with the 2 cords parallel and then pass the end of cord B behind cord A from right to left. Bring cord B around and over the top of cord A from left to right.

Step 2 Bend the bottom end of cord A upwards over the loop.

Step 3 Then fold the end of cord A between the upper ends of the cords, and down behind the loop.

Step 4 Take the bottom end of cord B and pass it behind cord A from right to left, and then up and through the vertical loop formed by cord A. Gently pull cord B.

Step 5 Tighten the knot into a neat cross by gently pulling all the cord ends.

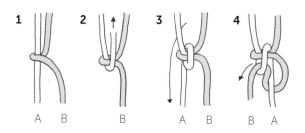

braids

Most of us know how to braid with 3 strands – it is something we can do intuitively without thinking about technique. If you add more strands to your braid, however, the level of difficulty increases. The 'conventional' method weaves both outer cords towards the centre, using different techniques for 4-, 5- or 6-ply braids. However, I find it easier to use a method where you always weave the left cord to the right, regardless of the number of strands.

3-ply braid 3-PB

The basic braid uses 3 strands. If you wish to make a thicker braid but don't want to add strands, simply add more cords per strand and use the same technique.

Step 1 Arrange your 3 strands parallel with each other and pass cord A to the right over cord B.

Step 2 Pass cord C to the left over cord A.

Step 3 Pass cord B to the right over cord C.

Step 4 Pass cord A to the left over cord B again.

Step 5 Continue braiding by taking the cord to the left over the centre cord, and then the cord to the right over the centre cord.

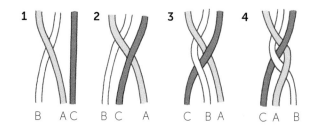

4-ply braid 4-PB

The 4-ply braid starts by crossing cords B and D right over left, passes cord A over D and under C, and then continues by always weaving the cord to the very left under, over and under again until it is on the very right. Make sure to keep the cords in the right order.

Step 1 Arrange your 4 strands parallel to each other. Pass cord B to the left over cord A, and cord D to the left over cord C.

Step 2 Continue weaving with cord A. Pass it to the right over cord D and then under cord C.

Step 3 Weave cord B all the way across. Pass it under cord D, over cord C, and then under cord A. Pull the weaving cord upwards to tighten the braid.

Step 4 Repeat the action in step 3, always using the cord to the very left and taking it under, over, and under until your braid is the desired length. You might need to pull each cord from time to time to keep tightening the braid.

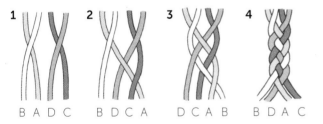

5-ply braid 5-PB

The 5-ply braid starts by crossing cord A over B and E over D. Cord A is then woven across to the right, and the braid continues by always weaving the cord to the very left across to the right. Make sure to keep the cords in the right order.

Step 1 Arrange your 5 strands parallel to each other and pass cord A to the right over cord B and pass cord E to the left over cord D.

Step 2 Continue weaving with cord A. Pass it to the right under cord C, over cord E and then under cord D to the very right.

Step 3 Now weave cord B all the way across. Pass it over cord C, under cord E, over cord D and then under cord A. Gently pull the weaving cord (B) upwards to tighten the braid, while holding the other cords straight.

Step 4 Repeat the action in step 3, always using the cord to the very left and taking it over, under, over, under until your braid is the desired length. You might need to pull each cord from time to time to keep tightening the braid.

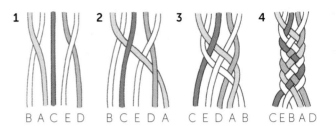

6-ply braid 6-PB

You might recognize this broad and intricate braid from belts. The 6-ply braid is a little more complex to begin with, but as you reach step 4, the technique is the same as for the 4- and 5-ply braid.

Step 1 Arrange your 6 strands parallel to each other and pass cord C to the right over cord D. Pass cord D to the left over cord B and pass cord E to the left over cord C.

Step 2 Cross cord B to the right over cord E.

Step 3 First, pass cord C to the right over cord F. Then continue weaving with cord B. Pass it to the right under cord F and then over cord C, to the very right.

Step 4 Now weave cord A all the way across. Pass it to the right over cord D, under cord E, over cord F, under cord C, and then over cord B. Gently pull the weaving cord (A) upwards to tighten the braid, while holding the other cords straight.

Step 5 Repeat the action in step 4, always using the cord to the very left and taking it over, under, over, under, over until your braid is the desired length. Make sure that the cords are always in the right order when you weave. You might need to pull the cords from time to time to keep tightening the braid.

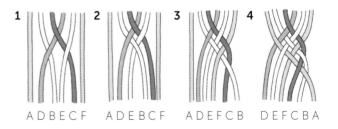

patterns

This section shows you the various ways of combining knots to create different patterns. Repeat or combine these patterns in wall hangings or other projects to make your own designs. When you try out the projects in this book, you will also get to practise some of these patterns.

arrows

These instructions are for a geometrical pattern using diagonal clove hitches. Each section (one half of the arrow) includes 7 clove hitches per row – so 8 cords including the filler cord. In other words, use any multiple of 8 cords to make the pattern as wide as you want.

Knots used
Diagonal clove hitch (DCH) page 22

instructions

Step 1 To begin tying the first arrow (cords 1–16), take the first cord on the left and use it as a filler cord to work 7 diagonal clove hitches (DCH) in towards the middle and pointing downwards. Then take the sixteenth cord and use it as a filler cord to work another 7 diagonal clove hitches into the middle and pointing downwards. Continue with 3 more rows, always using the cords to the very left and right as the filler cords. Repeat this for the remaining sets of 16 cords in your panel.

Step 2 Once you have finished the first 4 rows, use the left filler cord as a filler cord for another clove hitch in the middle to connect the arrow.

Step 3 Continue the pattern with another 4 rows of 7 diagonal clove hitches, this time working from the middle to the edge and pointing downwards.

Step 4 Repeat steps 2–3 until the pattern is the desired length.

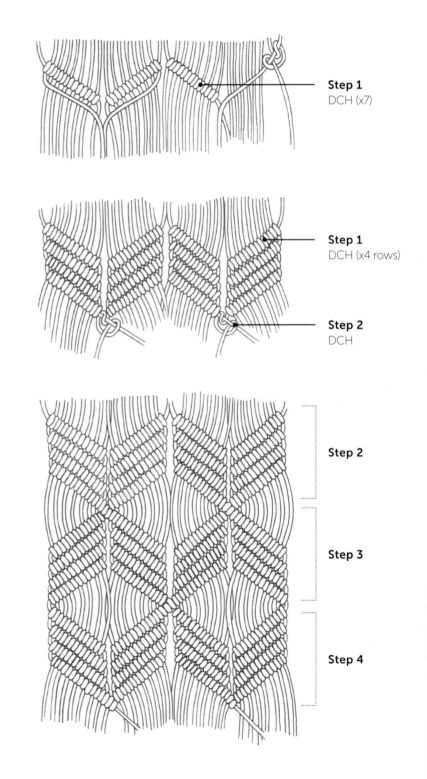

Step 1
DCH (x7)

Step 1
DCH (x4 rows)

Step 2
DCH

Step 2

Step 3

Step 4

fishbone

These instructions are to tie a fishbone pattern with 32 cords. Each section includes 5 square knots and uses 12 cords, while the half sections on the sides use 8 cords. If you wish to add or subtract square knots on each section, you just add or subtract one cord on each side. The filler cords are never used to tie any knots so they do not need to be extra-long, but the cords to the very left and right do since they are used the most for tying knots.

Knots used
Right-facing square knot (RFSK) page 18

instructions

Step 1 Make 3 square knots (SK) to begin the fishbone sections using cords 1–4, 15–18, and 29–32. To continue the sennit on the left side, continue with cord 1, but use cord 5 as the other working cord and the same 2 filler cords used to make the initial 3 square knots. On the right sennit, cords 32 and 28 are the working cords. For the middle sennit, use cords 14 and 19 to tie the next square knot.

Step 2 Finish the 3 first sennits of 5 square knots each by adding in new working cords for each new square knot. After you have tied the fifth square knot for all sennits, there should be 2 cords left loose between each of the sennits.

Step 3 To begin the second row of the fishbone pattern; take the working cords from the top of the previous row and tie a new knot around the 2 loose cords in the middle. Continue with the second square knot using the working cords from the second knot in the previous row. Continue with the 3 other cords.

Step 4 Repeat steps 1–3 until the pattern is the desired length.

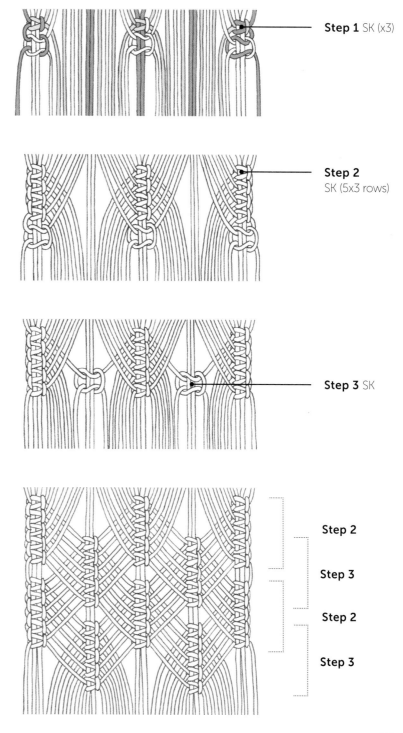

Step 1 SK (x3)

Step 2
SK (5x3 rows)

Step 3 SK

Step 2

Step 3

Step 2

Step 3

butterfly

These instructions are to tie a butterfly with 18 cords. To make the butterfly smaller or larger, add or subtract 2 cords at a time.

<u>Knots used</u>
Diagonal clove hitch (DCH) page 22
Right-facing square knot (RFSK) page 18
Left-facing square knot (LFSK) page 18

instructions

<u>Step 1</u> Cords 1 and 18 are your filler cords as you work a row of 8 diagonal clove hitches (DCH) on each side, from the edges into the middle. Tie 2 more rows of 8 diagonal clove hitches, placed directly underneath the first rows.

<u>Step 2</u> Using cords 3–6, tie a right-facing square knot (RFSK) under the clove hitches (in the upper left wing). Then use cords 13–16 to tie a left-facing square knot (LFSK) under the clove hitches (in the upper right wing).

<u>Step 3</u> Use cords 1 and 18 as filler cords to work a row of 8 diagonal clove hitches on each side, working from the edges into the middle, completing the upper wings.

<u>Step 4</u> Use the 4 middle cords (cords 8–11) to tie a right-facing square knot to connect the wings.

<u>Step 5</u> Use the working cords that created the middle square knot (cords 8 and 11) as filler cords to work a row of 7 diagonal clove hitches on each side, working from the middle to the edges.

<u>Step 6</u> Tie 2 rows of 8 diagonal clove hitches, placed directly underneath the first rows. Using cords 4–7, tie a right-facing square knot under the clove hitches (in the lower left wing). Using cords 12–15, tie a left-facing square knot under the clove hitches (in the lower right wing).

<u>Step 7</u> Complete the butterfly by tying a row of 8 diagonal clove hitches on each side, working from the middle to the edges.

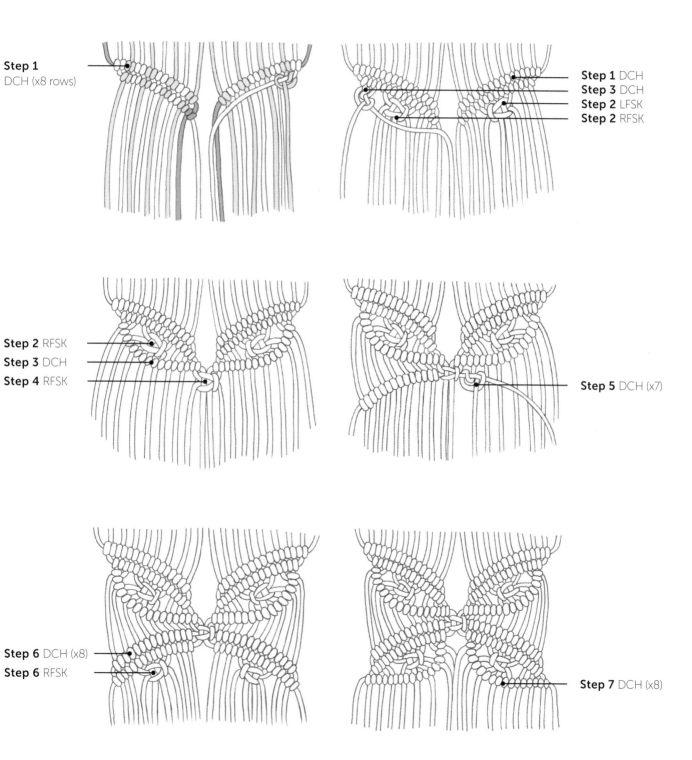

Step 1
DCH (x8 rows)

Step 1 DCH
Step 3 DCH
Step 2 LFSK
Step 2 RFSK

Step 2 RFSK
Step 3 DCH
Step 4 RFSK

Step 5 DCH (x7)

Step 6 DCH (x8)
Step 6 RFSK

Step 7 DCH (x8)

leaves

These instructions are to tie a pattern with leaves using 16 cords. The filler cord (cord 8) that runs through the 'stem' will not get much shorter as you knot, while the others will need plenty of extra length. Exactly how much depends on how long you want the stem with leaves to be, but somewhere between 3 to 5 times the length of the finished result. As always, this depends on how tight you tie the knots, and how long your fringes are.

<u>Knots used</u>
Diagonal clove hitch (DCH) page 22

instructions

<u>Step 1</u> Begin by tying 5 diagonal clove hitches (DCH) for the stem with cords 9–13, using cord 8 as the filler cord and working from left to right. Leave 3 loose cords to the right. To begin the first leaf, use cord 9 (used to make the second clove hitch of the stem) as the filler cord for the top part.

<u>Step 2</u> Tie 8 diagonal clove hitches for the top part of the leaf, working from right to left. There should be no loose cords on the left side – make sure you use all the cords on the left. Then take the cord used to make the first clove hitch of the top part of the leaf and lay it across to make the filler cord for the bottom part of the leaf.

<u>Step 3</u> Finish the bottom part of the leaf by tying another 8 diagonal clove hitches. Take the filler cord for the stem (which is now cord 13) and lay it across to the left. There should still be 3 loose cords to the right.

<u>Step 4</u> Try to make the diagonal into a bent shape. Tie 9 diagonal clove hitches from right to left to continue the stem. Leave 3 loose cords to the left. The eighth cord will be used as filler cord to make the top part of the second leaf.

<u>Step 5</u> Make the second leaf by tying 8 diagonal clove hitches for the upper part, and 8 diagonal clove hitches for the lower part. As for all the leaves, the working cord used for the first clove hitch of the upper part will be the filler cord for the bottom part of the leaf.

<u>Step 6</u> Continue the pattern by repeating the steps. Remember, the stem should always have 3 loose cords on each side. The left leaf should always use cords 1–9, with the ninth cord as the upper part of the filler cord. The right leaf should always use cords 8–16, with the eighth cord as the upper part of the filler cord.

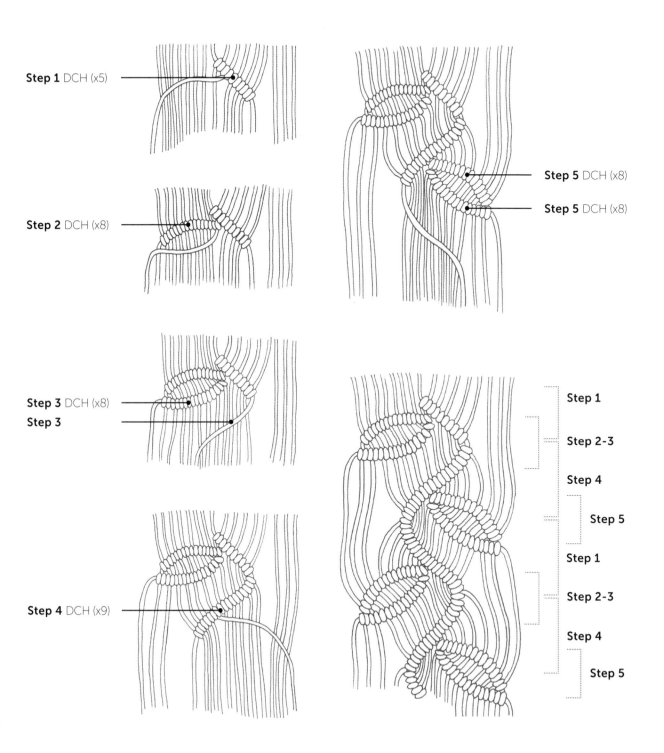

Step 1 DCH (x5)

Step 2 DCH (x8)

Step 3 DCH (x8)
Step 3

Step 4 DCH (x9)

Step 5 DCH (x8)
Step 5 DCH (x8)

Step 1
Step 2-3
Step 4
Step 5
Step 1
Step 2-3
Step 4
Step 5

triangles

These instructions show you one of the endless ways of combining alternating square knots to make a beautiful pattern – in this case by making triangles. Each triangle is made of 4 square knots at its widest point, so 16 cords per triangle – although you'll need at least 2 triangles across to get a symmetrical effect, so 32 cords minimum.

Knots used
Right-facing square knot (RFSK) page 18
Alternating square knot (ASK) page 19

instructions

Step 1 Begin tying 1 row of square knots (SK) across the panel using all cords. Continue by tying 3 alternating square knots (ASK) underneath each set of 4 knots. Place the knots close to the row above. Tie 2 more rows, one with 2 alternating square knots and one with 1 alternating square knot, to complete the first level of triangles.

Step 2 For the second level of triangles, tie another row of alternating square knots with all the cords. Make sure that they remain in a straight horizontal line. On the second row, begin with a half triangle at the edge with only 1 alternating square knot under the first 2. The following full triangles will all be offset to the previous level, ending with another half triangle. Continue with 2 more rows to complete the second level of triangles; on either edge the half triangles will only consist of 3 rows.

Step 3 Repeat steps 1 and 2 until you have the desired length.

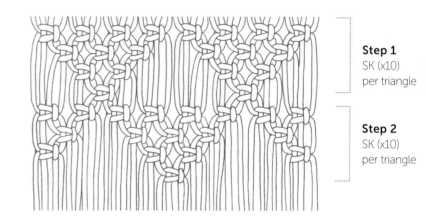

Step 1
SK (x10)
per triangle

Step 2
SK (x10)
per triangle

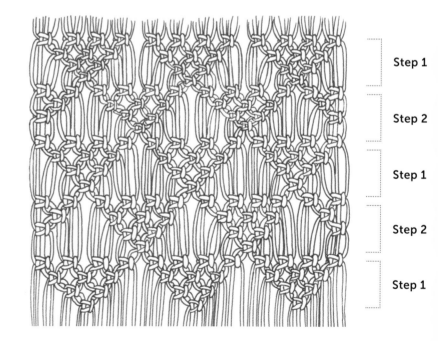

Step 1

Step 2

Step 1

Step 2

Step 1

Top (from left to right):
triangles and net
Bottom (from left to right):
arrows, leaves, butterfly

net

This is one of the most basic combinations of knots in macramé – tying alternating square knots to create a net. Depending on how far apart you place each row, you will either have a loose, airy net or a tight, compact net. It doesn't matter if you work with right-facing or left-facing square knots, but for a symmetrical design it is best if you are consistent and avoid switching between them.

Knots used

Alternating square knot (ASK) page 19
Right-facing square knot (RFSK) page 18

instructions

Tie the first row of square knots (SK) across the panel. For the rest of the rows, alternate the working cords and filler cords on each row to tie alternating square knots (ASK), making sure that the spaces between them are equal. Continue until a net is formed.

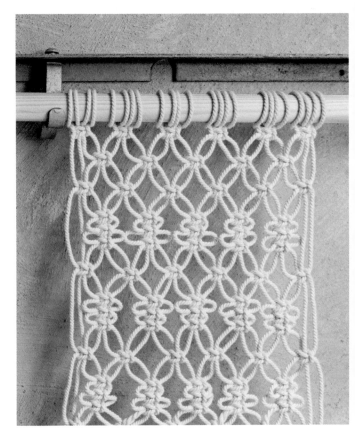

Picot net pattern

Tip

If you find it difficult to keep the rows straight, you can try using a bar, such as a ruler or a dowel, between the rows. Place the bar with the filler cords behind it and the working cords in front. Tie the knots 'around' the bar and once you have finished the row you can slide it out.

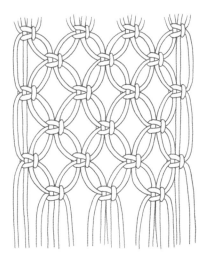

picot net

These instructions show you one way of incorporating the square knot picot design into a panel. Remember that the working cords will need to be much longer than if you were making a pattern with simple alternating square knots. You will need at least 8 cords to make this pattern.

Knots used
Alternating square knot (ASK) page 19
Picot square knot (PSK) page 19
Square knot (SK) page 18

instructions

Step 1 Begin with 1 row of square knots (SK). Continue with a second row of alternating square knots (ASK) spaced away from the row above. These are the first knots in the first sennits of 3 square knots each. Make a second square knot using the same working cords, leaving a little space between the first and second knots. Push the second knot up towards the first to make a picot square knot (PSK), placing it just underneath. The third square knot in the sennit is placed with a little more space between it and the second, so that when you push it up the picot will be slightly larger than the first one.

Step 2 Tie 2 more rows of alternating square knots, leaving a space between the rows. After the second row of square knots, continue with the same working and filler cords to make the 3-knot sennits, but now with the larger picots above and the smaller ones below.

Step 3 Repeat steps 1–2 until you have the desired length.

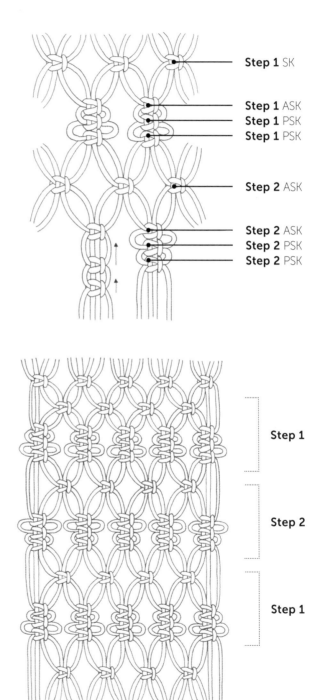

Step 1 SK

Step 1 ASK
Step 1 PSK
Step 1 PSK

Step 2 ASK

Step 2 ASK
Step 2 PSK
Step 2 PSK

Step 1

Step 2

Step 1

projects

Once you have mastered the techniques for the essential macramé knots, it is time for you to try making your very own macramé pieces. This section provides 21 different macramé projects for you to choose from, varying in style, size, and difficulty. You will find plenty of different designs for the typical macramé objects – plant hangers, wall hangings, and dreamcatchers. In addition, you will get to delve deeper into the art of macramé and apply it to other unique projects, such as a lantern, garland, and even a bench. Happy knotting!

candy cane
plant hanger

Dip dyeing plant hangers is super easy and looks so good! This 110-cm (43¼-in) long plant hanger has a loop at the top made out of rope, which is perfect if you don't have any metal or wooden rings at home.

Knots used

Square knot (SK) page 18
Right-twisting half square knot (RTHSK) page 20
Alternating square knot (ASK) page 19
4-ply crown knot (4-CK) page 25
Wrap knot (WK) page 23

Materials

42m (46 yd) of twined 4mm (³/₁₆ in) cotton rope
4 wooden beads, 2–2.5cm (³/₄–1 in) diameter with 6–10mm (¹/₄–³/₈ in) diameter hole

Equipment

Pink fabric dye
Brush

Preparation

Cut the following:
4 cords, each 3.4m (3³/₄ yd) long
2 cords, each 6m (6⁵/₈ yd) long
1 cord, 7.4m (8¹/₈ yd) long (extra-long to make the top loop)
1 cord, 8.6m (9¹/₂ yd) long (extra-long to make the top loop and the wrap knot at the end)

instructions

Step 1
Take the 4 3.4m (3³/₄ yd) cords and the 2 6m (6⁵/₈ yd) cords and lay them on the floor parallel to each other, with the middle point of each cord aligned. These cords will be used as filler cords in the top loop. Take the 2 remaining cords and place them on either side of the others, so both of them have one end aligned with the top end of the 2 6m (6⁵/₈ yd) long cords. These will be used as the working cords for the loop.

Step 2
Use the longer end of each working cord, which is not aligned with the other cords to tie a line of 11 square knots (SK) to make a sennit placed at the centre of the bundle of filler cords. Make sure you use the long ends of the working cords, and that the other ends remain aligned with the top ends of the 6m (6⁵/₈ yd) filler cords.

Step 3
Bend the sennit into a loop. Use the long end of the working cords to tie a spiral of right-twisting half square knots (RTHSK) around all the other cords. The spiral should be about 6cm (2³/₈ in) long, or about 10 to 15 half square knots.

Step 4
Divide the cords into 4 bundles, each containing 2 long cords and 2 short cords. Begin by tying each bundle into a sennit, each with 15 square knots.

Step 5
Drop about 10cm (4in) and tie a square knot in each of the bundles of cord. Thread a bead onto the 2 filler cords of each bundle, then tie another square knot underneath the bead.

Step 6
Under each square knot tie a spiral of right-twisting half square knots (RTHSK), each about 13cm (5¹/₈ in) long or 20 to 24 half square knots.

Step 7
To make the net, tie 2 rows of alternating square knots (ASK), alternating the filler cords and working cords. Place the knots with about 6–7cm (2³/₈–2³/₄ in) of space above and below them.

Step 8
To tie the cords together at the base, make a 4-ply crown knot (4-CK), using the 4 sets of cords as working cords as shown in the illustration. Place your fist on a table with the tail of the plant hanger held upside down, and lay the cords down to make it easier to work the crown knot. Place the crown knot about 6–7cm (2³/₈–2³/₄ in) from the square knots above it. Tie 5 to 6 rounds of the crown knot.

Step 9
Take the longest remaining cord and tie a 5–6cm (2–2³/₈ in) long wrap knot (WK) around all the other cords.

Step 10
The plant hanger is now finished except for the dip dyeing! Follow the instructions on the package to make up the dip dye, and then place just the tail of the plant hanger in the dye and allow it to soak up as much colour as you want. If you want frayed ends, fray and brush them before you dip the plant hanger, otherwise the colour won't soak through the thickness of the cords.

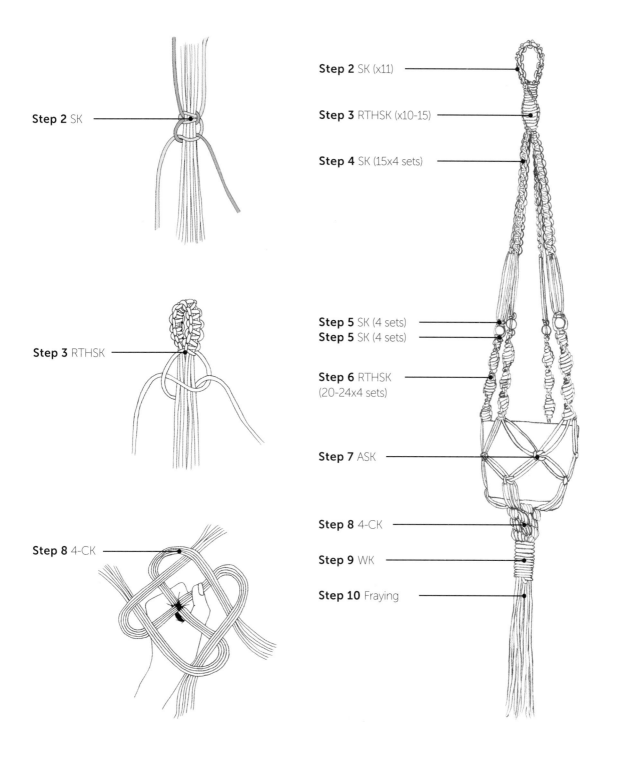

Step 2 SK

Step 3 RTHSK

Step 8 4-CK

Step 2 SK (x11)

Step 3 RTHSK (x10-15)

Step 4 SK (15x4 sets)

Step 5 SK (4 sets)
Step 5 SK (4 sets)

Step 6 RTHSK
(20-24x4 sets)

Step 7 ASK

Step 8 4-CK

Step 9 WK

Step 10 Fraying

honey bee
plant hanger

This 120cm (47¼in) long plant hanger gets its name from the picot knots combined with the yellow rope which makes me think of small insect wings! You can also switch to use alternating square knots here.

Knots used

Overhand knot (OK) page 18
Wrap knot (WK) page 24
Square knot (SK) page 18
Square knot sennit (SK sennit) page 18
Picot square knot (PSK) page 19
Josephine knot (JK) page 26
4-ply crown knot (4-CK) page 25

Materials

38m (41⅝yd) of twined 2.5mm (⅛in) cotton rope
Wooden ring, 4–5cm (1½–2in) diameter
8 wooden beads, 2–2.5cm (¾–1in) diameter with 6–10mm (¼–⅜in) diameter hole

Equipment

Brush
Crochet hook (to help thread the beads)

Preparation

Cut the following:
4 cords, each 3m (3¼yd) long (filler cords)
3 cords, each 6m (6⅝yd) long (working cords)
1 cord, 8m (8¾yd) long (extra-long to make the wrap knots)

instructions

Pair a 3m (3¹/₄ yd) cord with a 6m (6⁵/₈ yd) cord. Pass them through the ring, folding both in the middle, then bundle the 4 cords together with an overhand knot (OK) to keep them from falling out or moving in the ring. Repeat with the remaining cords, except for one 3m (3¹/₄ yd) filler cord and the extra-long working cord. Pass the last filler cord and the extra-long working cord through the ring and fold both in the middle. Bundle together both ends of the filler cord with one end of the extra-long working cord using an overhand knot, and leaving the other long end loose.

Step 1
Using the loose extra-long working cord, make a 4–5cm (1¹/₂–2in) long wrap knot (WK) just underneath the ring, gathering all the other cords together.

Step 2
Untie the overhand knot (OK) with only 3 ends, and add in the cord you used to make the wrap knot. Use both long cords to tie a sennit of 17 square knots (SK). Untie the other overhand knots one at a time and tie 17 square knots with each set of cords.

Step 3
Tie 2 picot square knots (PSK). Thread the filler cords through a bead (you might need the help of a crochet hook or tapestry needle), then tie 2 more picot square knots under the bead. Repeat for the other 3 sets of cords.

Step 4
Tie another sennit of 6 square knots and repeat for the other 3 sets of cords.

Step 5
Tie 3 picot square knots. Thread the filler cords through a bead, then tie 3 more picot square knots under the bead. Repeat for the other 3 sets of cords.

Step 6
Tie another sennit of 9 square knots and repeat for the other 3 sets of cords.

Step 7
Take a filler cord and a working cord from 2 sennits and tie a Josephine knot (JK), placed about 10 cm (4in) from the sennits above. Tie 3 more Josephine knots to finish the net.

Step 8
To tie the cords together, make a 4-ply crown knot (4-CK), using the 4 sets of cords as working cords, as shown in the illustration. Place your fist on a table with the tail of the plant hanger held upside down, and lay the cords down to make it easier to work the crown knot. Place the crown knot about 10cm (4in) from the Josephine knots above it. Tie 5 to 6 rounds of the crown knot.

Step 9
Take the longest remaining cord and tie a 4–5cm (1¹/₂–2in) long wrap knot around all other cords.

Step 10
Fray all the ends and use a brush to give the tail more volume.

Start OK (4 sets)

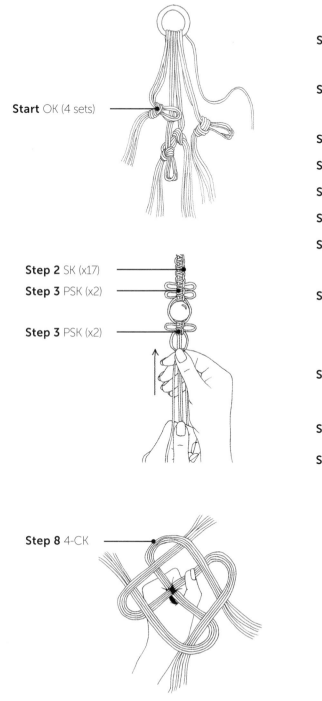

Step 2 SK (x17)

Step 3 PSK (x2)

Step 3 PSK (x2)

Step 8 4-CK

Step 1 WK

Step 2 SK (17x4 sets)

Step 3 PSK (2x4 sets)

Step 3 PSK (2x4 sets)

Step 4 SK (6x4 sets)

Step 5 PSK (3x4 sets)

Step 5 PSK (3x4 sets)

Step 6 SK (9x4 sets)

Step 7 JK

Step 8 4-CK

Step 9 WK

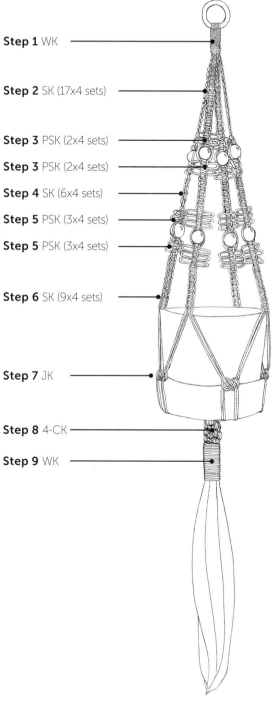

flora
plant hanger

This 140cm (55$^{1}/_{8}$ in) double plant hangers is the perfect way bring more plants into your home! It's made the same way as a single plant hanger, but after the crown knot you repeat the knotting as though you are making another plant hanger.

Knots used
Overhand knot (OK) page 18
Wrap knot (WK) page 24
Right-twisting half square knots (RTHSK) page 20
Square knot (SK) page 18
Alternating square knot (ASK) page 19
4-ply crown knot (4-CK) page 25

Materials
45m (49$^{1}/_{4}$ yd) of twined 2.5mm ($^{1}/_{8}$ in) cotton rope
Wooden ring, 4–5cm (1$^{1}/_{2}$–2in) diameter
8 wooden beads, 2–2.5cm ($^{3}/_{4}$–1in) diameter with
6–10mm ($^{1}/_{4}$–$^{3}/_{8}$ in) diameter hole

Equipment
Crochet hook or tapestry needle (to help thread the beads)

Preparation
Cut the following:
4 cords, each 4m (4$^{3}/_{8}$ yd) long (filler cords)
3 cords, each 6.8m (7$^{1}/_{2}$ yd) long (working cords)
1 cord, 8m (8$^{3}/_{4}$ yd) long (extra-long working cord, also used for wrap knots)

Pair a 4m (4$^{3}/_{8}$ yd) cord with a 6.8m (7$^{1}/_{2}$ yd) cord. Pass them through the ring, folding both in the middle, then bundle the 4 cords together with an overhand knot to keep them from falling out or moving in the ring. Repeat with the remaining cords, except for one 4m (4$^{3}/_{8}$ yd) filler cord and the extra-long working cord. Pass the last filler cord and the extra-long working cord through the ring and fold both in the middle. Bundle together both ends of the filler cord with one end of the extra-long working cord using an overhand knot (OK) and leaving the other long end loose.

instructions

Step 1

Using the loose extra-long working cord, make a 3–4cm (1⅛–1½ in) long wrap knot (WK) just underneath the ring, gathering all the other cords together.

Step 2

Untie the overhand knot with only 3 ends and add in the cord you used to make the wrap knot. Use both long cords to tie right-twisting half square knots (RTHSK), forming an 18cm (7in) spiral.

Step 3

Tie a square knot (SK) 4cm (1½ in) under the spiral.

Step 4

Pass the 2 filler cords through a bead (you might need the help of a crochet hook or a tapestry needle). Tie another square knot with the working cords, placing it underneath the bead.

Step 5

Leave a gap of 4cm (1½ in) and tie a 8cm (3⅛ in) spiral using right-twisting half square knots.

Step 6

Untie the other overhand knots and repeat steps 2–5 for the other 3 sets of cords in turn.

Step 7

Beginning 6cm (2⅜ in) under the spirals, tie a row of alternating square knots (ASK) using the filler cords from adjacent sets of cords. When you are done, the 4 sets will be tied together in a net-like shape. Under each alternating square knot, tie 2 more square knots, making 3 in a row.

Step 8

Take the 4 separate sets of cords (4 cords in each set) and tie them together with an overhand knot to make the 4-ply crown knot (CK) easier.

Step 9

Tie 3 rounds of the crown knot, beginning 6cm (2⅜ in) below the last alternating square knot. See the illustrations on page 49 for how best to hold the cords when tying the crown knot.

Step 10

Begin the second part of the plant hanger by untying one set of cords and tying an 8cm (3⅛ in) spiral under the crown knot, using the long cords as working cords.

Step 11

Tie a square knot 4cm (1½ in) below the spiral. Pass the filler cords through a bead, and tie another square knot under it.

Step 12

Beginning 4cm (1½ in) below the square knot, tie another 8cm (3⅛ in) spiral.

Step 13

Repeat steps 10–12 for the other 3 sets of cords.

Step 14

Tie a row of alternating square knots using the filler cords from adjacent sets of cords, as you did in step 7 but beginning 8cm (3⅛ in) below the spiral to allow for a slightly larger pot. Tie 3 more square knots under each alternating square knot, making 4 in a row.

Step 15

Separate each set of cords (4 cords in each set) and tie them together with overhand knots to make the crown knot easier. Tie 5 rounds of the crown knot, beginning 6cm (2⅜ in) below the alternating square knots.

Step 16

Finish by making a 5cm (2in) tall wrap knot under the crown knot, using the longest remaining cord. Cut the cords to the same length, if you wish, and fray the ends.

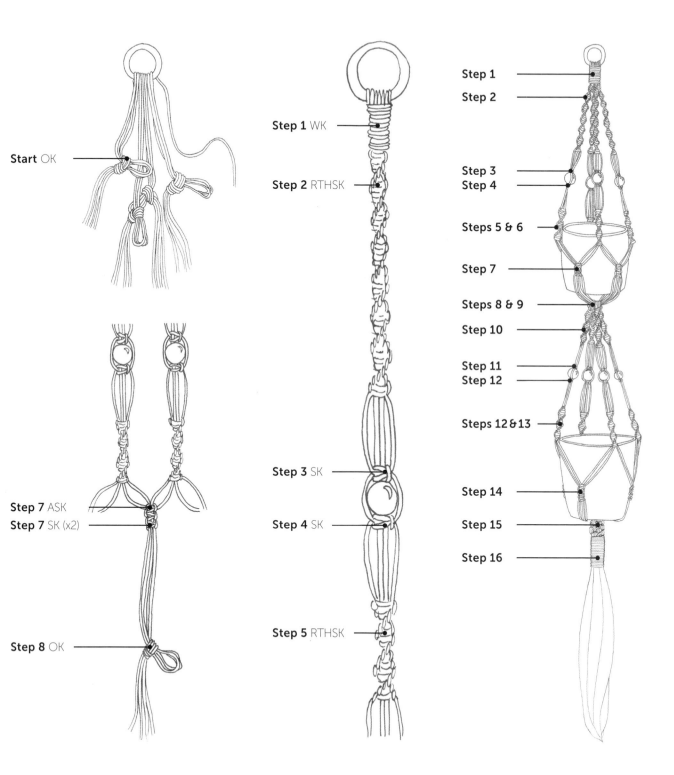

Start OK

Step 7 ASK
Step 7 SK (x2)

Step 8 OK

Step 1 WK

Step 2 RTHSK

Step 3 SK

Step 4 SK

Step 5 RTHSK

Step 1
Step 2

Step 3
Step 4

Steps 5 & 6

Step 7

Steps 8 & 9

Step 10

Step 11
Step 12

Steps 12 & 13

Step 14

Step 15

Step 16

agatha
plant hanger

This is an alternative plant hanger design that can be hung on a wall. It starts out as a wall hanging (so the pattern can also be used to make a plain hanging), and ends with the bottom part of a plant hanger. The upper part can, of course, be changed to a different pattern if you prefer. The pattern given here will create a 12cm (4³/₄in) wide and 75cm (29¹/₂in) long plant hanger, which can hold a small pot of around 10–12cm (4–4³/₄in) in diameter.

Knots used
Reverse Lark's head knot (RLHK) page 21
Diagonal clove hitch (DCH) page 22
Square knot (SK) page 18
Alternating square knot (ASK) page 19
Wrap knot (WK) page 23

Materials
42m (46 yd) of twined or braided 2.5mm (¹/₈ in) cotton rope
30cm (11³/₄in) wooden dowel

Preparation
Cut the following:
11 cords, each 3.4m (3³/₄ yd) long
1 cord, 4m (4³/₈ yd) long

Fold each 3.4m (3³/₄ yd) cord in half and attach it to the dowel, using a reverse lark's head knot (RLHK). Fold the 4m (4³/₈ yd) cord with 1.7m (1⁷/₈ yd) to the left and 2.3m (2¹/₂ yd) to the right, and attach it anywhere to the dowel using a reverse lark's head knot. There are 12 cords used to create each of the two sections of this pattern, and the 8 middle cords are used to tie the two sections together using alternating square knots.

instructions

Step 1
Take cords 6 and 19 into the centre as filler cords for the first row of diagonal clove hitches (DCH). On the left section, use cord 7 to tie a diagonal clove hitch to the right on cord 6, and on the right section use cord 18 to tie a diagonal clove hitch to the left on cord 19. Continue in sequence to knot cords 8 to 12 onto cord 6, and cords 13 to 17 onto cord 19, working towards the middle, to make a row of 6 diagonal clove hitches on each side.

Step 2
Now use cords 6 and 19 as filler cords for the next diagonal, working down in the opposite direction, towards the edges.

Step 3
Work a second row of 4 diagonal clove hitches in each direction. Tie a third row with 3 diagonal clove hitches in each direction. Now take cords 1, 12, 13 and 24 as filler cords, bending 1 and 12 towards each other, and 13 and 24 towards each other. Work 5 diagonal clove hitches for each. To enclose the pattern, use cords 1 and 24 as filler cords, and 12 and 13 as working cords for one diagonal clove hitch per pair.

Step 4
Take the 4 cords in the middle (cords 11–14) and tie a square knot (SK) to tie the 2 sections together. Tie 2 alternating square knots (ASK) underneath the first square knot, and finish the merging section with another square knot underneath.

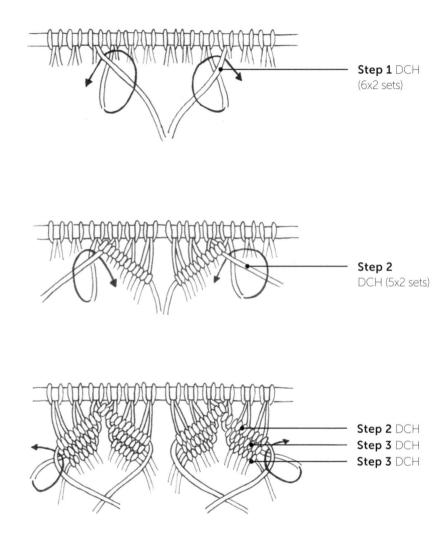

Step 1 DCH (6x2 sets)

Step 2 DCH (5x2 sets)

Step 2 DCH
Step 3 DCH
Step 3 DCH

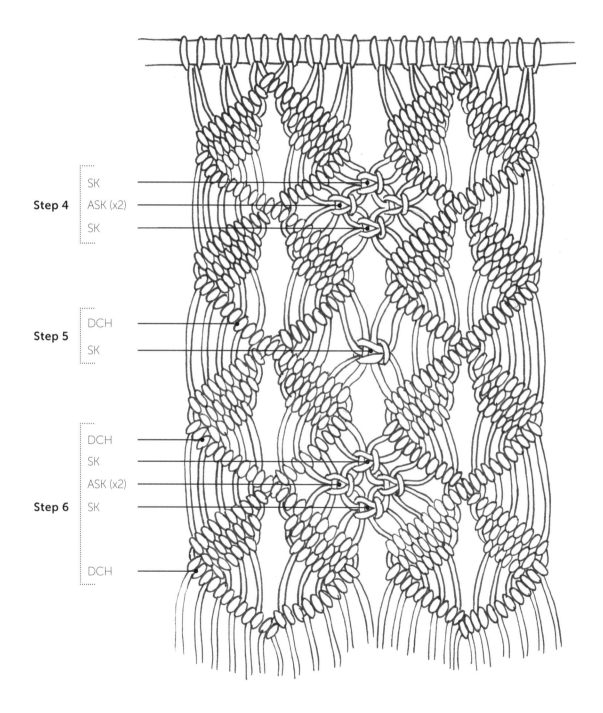

Step 4
SK
ASK (x2)
SK

Step 5
DCH
SK

Step 6
DCH
SK
ASK (x2)
SK

DCH

Step 5

Repeat steps 1–4, but only make 1 square knot to tie the sections together.

Step 6

Repeat steps 1–4 once more, and finish the upper part of the plant hanger by repeating steps 1–3.

Step 7

To make the net for the plant hanger, tie 2 rows of square knots using 8 cords for each knot, as shown in the illustration. For the first row, tie 3 square knots about 4–5cm (1$^{1}/_{2}$–2in) from the clove hitches above.

Step 8

For the second row, tie 2 alternating square knots 6cm (2$^{3}/_{8}$in) from the first row.

Step 9

To finish the net, take the 4 cords from each side and tie the last alternating square knot in front of the second row and about 3cm (1$^{1}/_{8}$in) lower than the 2 knots of the second row.

Step 10

Finish the plant hanger by taking the longer cord and tying a 4cm (1$^{1}/_{2}$in) long wrap knot around all the other cords. The wrap knot (WK) should begin about 9cm (3$^{1}/_{2}$in) from the 2 square knots at the back, and 6cm (2$^{3}/_{8}$in) from the square knot at the front. Cut the cords to the same length, if you wish, and fray the ends.

Tip

You may need to adjust the sets of cords in the wrap knot to get the knot in the middle underneath a pot. Put a small pot in the net and pull the 3 sets of cords either up through the wrap knot, or down through it, to tighten them.

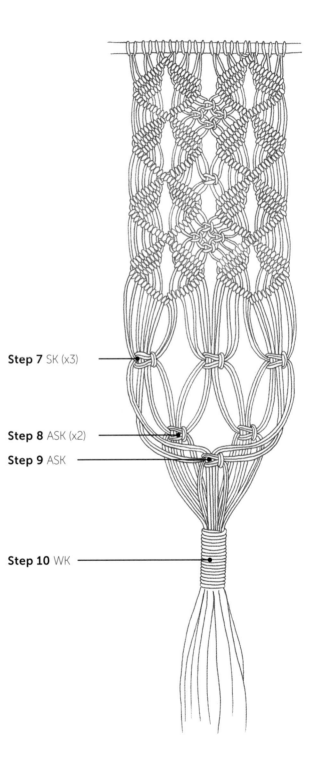

Step 7 SK (x3)

Step 8 ASK (x2)

Step 9 ASK

Step 10 WK

josephine
plant hanger

This is a different way to make a flat plant hanger to hang against a wall, with a looser, airier pattern. It's 115cm (45¼in) long and has a bohemian touch – this design work really well against a coloured wall.

Knots used
Reverse Lark's head knot (RLHK) page 20
Alternating half hitch (AHH) page 23
Right-twisting half square knots (RTHSK) page 20
Left-twisting half square knots (LTHSK) page 20
Square knot (SK) page 18
Square knots sennit (SK Sennit) page 18
Right-facing square knots (RFSK) page 18
Left-facing square knots (LFSK) page 18
Josephine knot (JK) page 26
Wrap knot (WK) page 23

Materials
30m (32³/₈ yd) of twined or braided 4mm (³/₁₆ in) cotton rope
40cm (15³/₄ in) piece of driftwood or a wooden dowel

Preparation
Cut the following:
2 cords, each 4m (4³/₈ yd) long
6 cords, each 3.6m (4yd) longx

Fold all the cords in half and attach to the driftwood using reverse lark's head knots (RLHK), with the six 3.6m (4yd) cords between the two 4m (4³/₈ yd) cords.

instructions

Step 1

Tie 8 alternating half hitch knots (AHH), using cords 1 and 2 on the left, and cords 15 and 16 on the right. Place the first knots 7cm (2 3/4 in) down from the reverse lark's head knots.

Step 2

Using cords 3 to 6, tie 6 right-twisting half square knots (RTHSK), 5cm (2 in) down from the lark's head knots. Repeat using cords 11 to 14, but make left-twisting half square knots (LTHSK).

Step 3

Using cords 7 to 10, tie a sennit of 4 square knots (SK).

Step 4

Use cords 4 to 7 as filler cords and cords 3 and 8 as working cords to tie a right-facing square knot (RFSK) 4cm (1 1/2 in) from the knots above. Repeat using cords 9 to 14, but making a left-facing square knot (LFSK).

Step 5

With cords 8 and 9 (the middle cords), tie a Josephine knot (JK), placed 4cm (1 1/2 in) from the square knots above.

Step 6

Beginning 5cm (2 in) from the alternating half hitches, tie an 11cm (4 1/4 in) spiral on both sides. Use cords 1 to 4 to make right-twisting half square knots, and cords 13 to 16 to make left-twisting half square knots.

Step 7

Beginning 5cm (2 in) from the Josephine knot, use cords 5 to 8 to tie a right-facing square knot, and cords 9 to 12 for a left-facing square knot.

Step 8

Tie a second Josephine knot 2cm (3/4 in) down from the square knots, using cords 7 to 10.

Step 9

Drop another 2cm (3/4 in), and tie a right-facing square knot using cords 5 to 8, and a left-facing square knot using cords 9 to 12.

Step 10

Drop another 2cm (3/4 in) and tie a third Josephine knot using cords 8 and 9.

Step 11

Take cords 4 and 13 from the half square spirals on each side and middle cords 8 and 9, and use them as working cords. With cords 5–7 and 10–12 as filler cords, tie a right-facing square knot on the left and a left-facing square knot on the right, beginning 2cm (3/4 in) from the Josephine knot above.

Step 12

Drop 5cm (2 in) and tie a right-facing square knot using cords 5 and 12, with cords 6 to 11 as filler cords.

Step 13

Tie a right-facing square knot with cords 1 to 4 and a left-facing square knot with cords 13 to 16, placing them 5cm (2 in) from the square knot above.

Step 14

Drop down another 8cm (3 1/8 in) and tie 3 square knots adjacent to each other, using cords 3 to 6, 7 to 10, and 11 to 14.

Step 15

To make the net for the plant, tie a square knot in front of the other cords, using cords 2 and 15 as working cords and 1 and 16 as filler cords. Place it 5cm (2 in) from the 3 square knots above.

Step 16

Finish the plant hanger by using the longest cord to tie a wrap knot (WK) around all the other cords. Hold the cords so that the last 4 square knots are all at the same level, making the front square looser than the 3 on the back. Cut the cords to the desired length below the wrap knot.

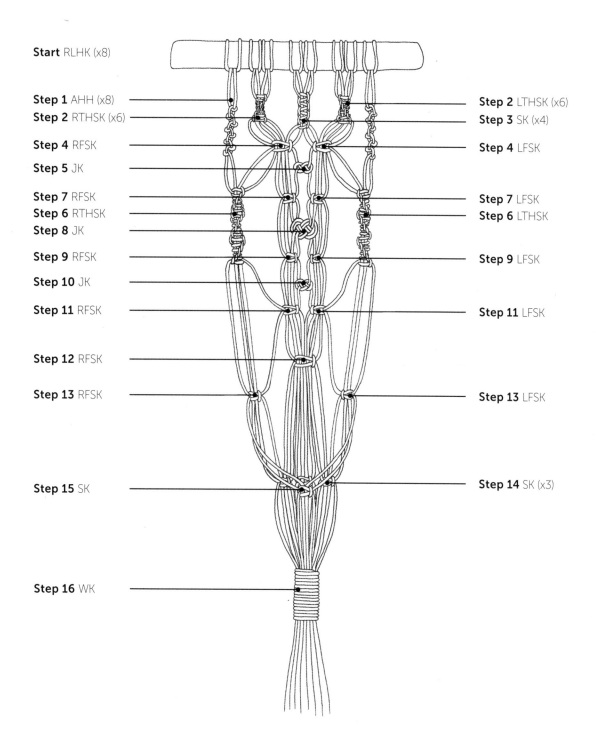

Start RLHK (x8)

Step 1 AHH (x8)

Step 2 RTHSK (x6)

Step 2 LTHSK (x6)

Step 3 SK (x4)

Step 4 RFSK

Step 4 LFSK

Step 5 JK

Step 7 RFSK

Step 7 LFSK

Step 6 RTHSK

Step 6 LTHSK

Step 8 JK

Step 9 RFSK

Step 9 LFSK

Step 10 JK

Step 11 RFSK

Step 11 LFSK

Step 12 RFSK

Step 13 RFSK

Step 13 LFSK

Step 15 SK

Step 14 SK (x3)

Step 16 WK

wilma
wall hanging

This little wall hanging is 22cm (8³/₄in) wide and 75cm (29¹/₂in) long. The pattern is very easy to make and to mould according to your own preferences. You can add more cords to make it wider, or add more beads – this is a style to play around with!

Knots used
Reverse lark's head knot (RLHK) page 21
Horizontal clove hitch (HCH) page 22

Materials
56m (60¹/₂yd) of twined 2.5mm (¹/₈in) cotton rope
40cm (15³/₄in) wooden stick or dowel
7 wooden beads, 2cm (³/₄in) diameter

Preparation
Cut the following:
18 cords, each 2.8m (3¹/₈yd) long
1 cord, 3.9m (4¹/₄yd) long (extra-long to use as filler cord for the horizontal clove hitches)

Fold each of the 18 cords in half and attach to the dowel using a reverse lark's head knot (RLHK). Fold the extra-long cord with 140cm (55in) on the left side and 250cm (98in) on the right, and attach it to the right of the other cords using a reverse lark's head knot.

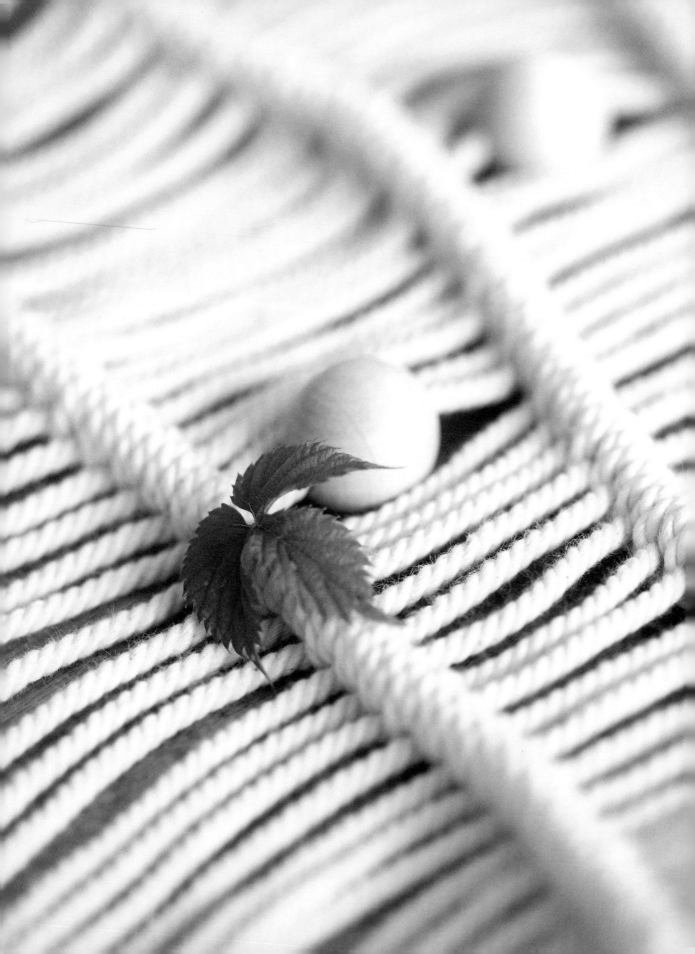

instructions

Step 1

Tie the first row of 37 horizontal clove hitches (HCH) from right to left, using the extra-long cord as filler cord. Place the knots just underneath the stick or dowel.

Step 2

To make the second row, place the filler cord across the body of the work in the position you would like the clove hitches to be and tie another row of horizontal clove hitches from left to right. When you reach the 26th cord (12th from the right), slide the first bead onto it then make a horizontal clove hitch beneath it. Carry on to finish the second row.

Step 3

For the third, fifth and seventh rows, the bead is placed on the 12th cord from the left (not counting the filler cord). On the fourth and sixth rows the bead is again placed on the 26th cord from the left (not counting the filler cord).

Step 4

For the last row, the bead is placed on the 19th cord from the left (not counting the filler cord).

Step 5

Cut the ends so they are the same length.

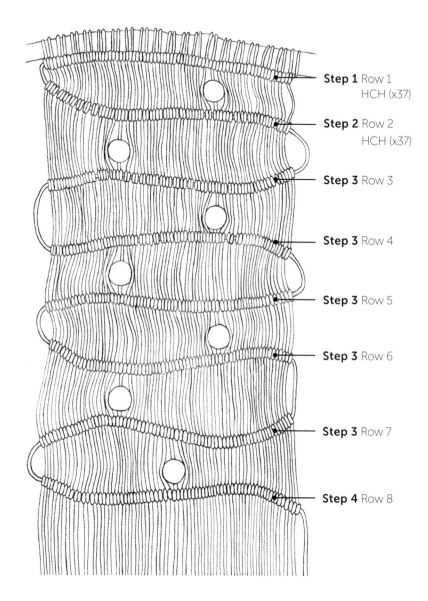

Step 1 Row 1
HCH (x37)

Step 2 Row 2
HCH (x37)

Step 3 Row 3

Step 3 Row 4

Step 3 Row 5

Step 3 Row 6

Step 3 Row 7

Step 4 Row 8

indra
wall hanging

This easy-to-make, yet attractive, wall hanging is 75cm (29^1/$_2$ in) high and 22cm (8^3/$_4$ in) wide and uses a repeat pattern that can be extended to make it wider or longer.

Knots used
Lark's head knot (LHK) page 20
Right-facing square knot (RFSK) page 18
Alternating square knot (ASK) page 19
Overhand knot (OK) page 18

Materials
51m (55^1/$_4$ yd) of twined or braided 2.5mm (^{1}/$_8$ in) cotton rope
35cm (14 in) wooden dowel
Tape

Preparation
Cut the following:
18 cords, each 2.8m (3^1/$_8$ yd) long

Tape the ends of your cords to keep them from fraying. Fold each cord in half and attach it to the dowel using a lark's head knot (LHK).

The chart (see page 71) for this wall hanging is divided into five sections. When section five is completed, the pattern repeats sections two to five until you have finished the pattern, ending with a repeat of sections two and three. To separate each section, leave a little space between the alternating square knots (about 6mm/^{1}/$_4$ in).

instructions

Step 1

For the first section, tie 2 right-facing square knots (RFSK) using the first 4 cords, skip 4 cords and then tie another 2 right-facing square knots using the next 4 cords, repeating this sequence to the end of the row. Then tie 1 right-facing square knot on each set of 4 cords that you skipped the first time, a total of 14 square knots.

Step 2

For the second section, skip the 2 first cords, then tie an alternating square knot (ASK) with every set of 4 cords. Skip the 2 last cords, to make a total of 8 square knots. Underneath each of these knots, tie another right-facing square knot to create a row of 8 sennits with 2 right-facing square knots in each.

Step 3

For the third section, skip the first 4 cords, then tie an alternating square knot with the next 4 cords, skip the next 4 cords, tie another alternating square knot with the next 4 cords, repeating this sequence to the end of the row, to make 4 square knots. Underneath each of these knots, tie 2 more right-facing square knots to create a row of 4 sennits with 3 right-facing square knots in each.

Step 4

For the fourth section, skip the 2 first cords, then tie an alternating square knot with every set of 4 cords and a right-facing square knot beneath (the same as in step 2), a total of 16 square knots.

Step 5

For the fifth section, tie an alternating square knot with the first 4 cords, then tie 2 more right-facing square knots directly beneath it to create a sennit of 3 right-facing square knots. Make a right-facing square knot with the next 4 cords, placing it at the same level as the middle knot of the previous 3 knots. Repeat this sequence to the end of the row, a total of 19 square knots.

Step 6

Repeat sections 2–5 2 more times, then tie sections 2 and 3 once more.

Step 7

Cut all the cords to the same length, then tie decorative overhand knots (OK) at the bottom of each cord. Fray the end of the cords beneath each knot to get a tassel effect.

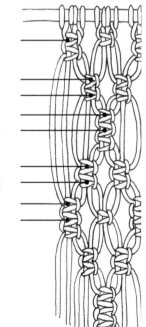

Step 1 RFSK

Step 2 ASK
Step 2 RFSK

Step 3 ASK
Step 3 RFSK

Step 4 ASK
Step 4 RFSK

Step 5 ASK
Step 5 RFSK

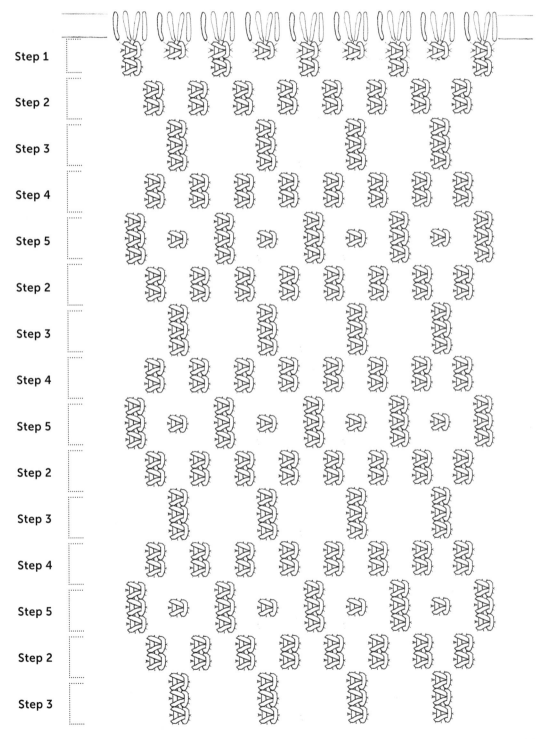

Step 1

Step 2

Step 3

Step 4

Step 5

Step 2

Step 3

Step 4

Step 5

Step 2

Step 3

Step 4

Step 5

Step 2

Step 3

atlantis
wall hanging

This wall hanging is 70cm (28 in) wide and 65cm (25⅝ in) long. Here, the main focus is less on the knots and more about the striking coloured fringe. Dip-dyeing your wall hanging allows you to do less knotting but still end up with an amazing piece – and you also save on material! In this project, cords are only attached to the branch in six places, while the rest are attached to these cords. If you have a beautiful branch, this is the perfect way of showing it off, otherwise this project also works well with a copper rod or wooden dowel!

Knots used
Lark's head knot (LHK) page 20
Horizontal clove hitch (HCH) page 22

Materials
81m (87¾ yd) of twined 4mm (³/₁₆ in) cotton rope
Wooden branch or dowel, at least 80cm (31½ in) long

Equipment
Blue fabric dye

Preparation
Cut the following:
2 cords, each 2.6m (2⅞ yd) long
24 cords, each 140cm (55 in) long
1 cord, 3m (3¼ yd) long
24 cords, each 160cm (63 in) long

instructions

Step 1

Take a 2.6m (2⁷/₈ yd) cord and attach it to the branch towards the left-hand end, using 2 lark's head knots (LHK). Leave a space between the knots of about 12–15cm (4³/₄–6in), and the loose cord ends on each side should be of equal length. Repeat with the other 2.6m (2⁷/₈ yd) cord, tying it on towards the right-hand end of the branch.

Step 2

Fold 12 of the 140cm (55 in) long cords in half and attach them onto one of the hanging loops from the previous step, using lark's head knots. If you need to, you can adjust the loose ends so that there is no space between the attached cords. Repeat on the other side with the remaining 140cm (55 in) long cords.

Step 3

Working on the left-hand end of the branch, take the loose end on either side and use it as a filler cord to work horizontal clove hitches (HCH) underneath the lark's head knots, working from each end into the middle. Work 12 clove hitches on each side. Repeat for the right-hand end of the branch.

Step 4

Go back to the left-hand end of the branch, and continue with the right filler cord, using it as filler cord again to work another 13 horizontal clove hitches going to the left in a slight U-shape. Use the left filler cord as working cord to make the first of the 13 clove hitches going to the right, to fasten the 2 sides together. Try to form a slight U-shaped curve with the clove hitches. Now take the filler cord that you used to make the middle clove hitch, and use it as filler cord to tie another 12 clove hitches going from the middle to the right. Repeat on the right-hand end of the branch, but begin with the left filler cord going to the right.

Step 5

To begin the middle section of the wall hanging, take the 3m (3¹/₄ yd) cord and attach it to the branch using 2 lark's head knots, positioning the knots so the middle section is in front of and overlaps the ends of the 2 side sections, as shown in the illustration. The loose ends on both sides should be of equal length.

Step 6

Fold all the 160cm (63 in) long cords in half and attach them to the hanging loop of the middle section, using lark's head knots. If you need to, you can adjust the loose ends so that there is no space between the attached cords. You can also move the 2 sections you have finished to place them at a good distance from each other on the branch.

Step 7

Repeat steps 3 and 4 for the middle section of the wall hanging.

Step 8

Finish the middle section by working 2 more rows of horizontal clove hitches, each going from the middle out to the edges, a total of 24 clove hitches on both sides.

Step 9

Cut the cords as you wish to make a nice fringe.

Step 10

Prepare the dye following the instructions on the package. Dip as much of the wall hanging as you feel like! See page 13 for tips on dip-dyeing.

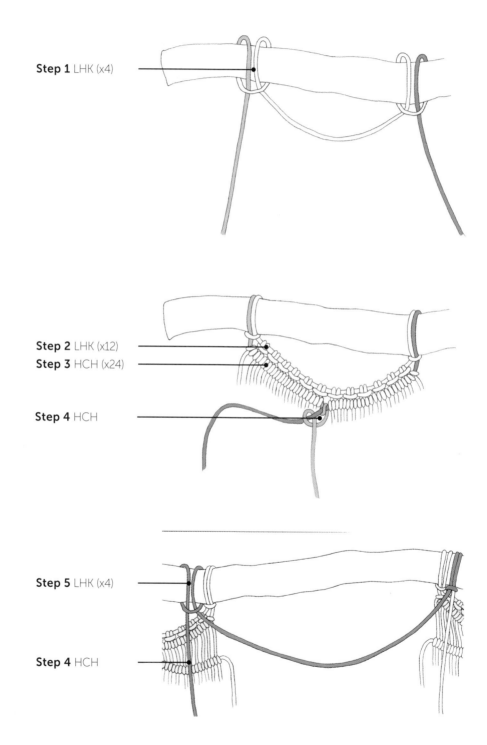

Step 1 LHK (x4)

Step 2 LHK (x12)
Step 3 HCH (x24)

Step 4 HCH

Step 5 LHK (x4)

Step 4 HCH

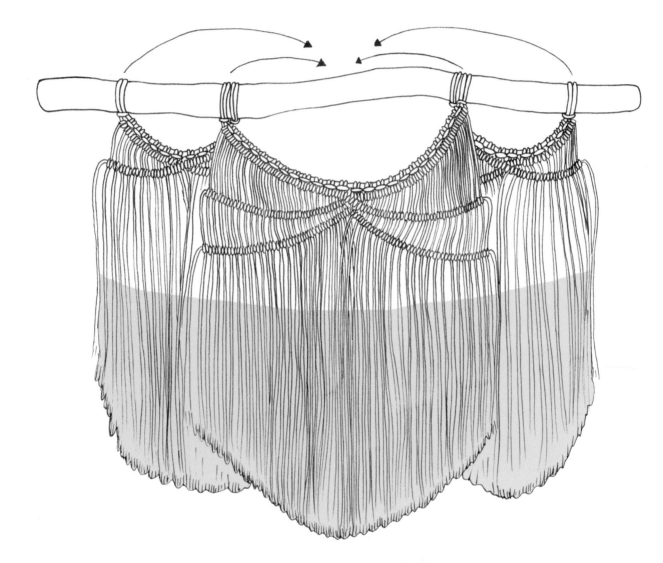

Tip
In order to dye the cords in a straight line, push all the cords on the branch towards the middle. Then tie all the cords together and dip them as a whole bundle. As the cords dry, move them back to their original places on the branch.

audrey
wall hanging

This wall hanging is 35cm (14 in) wide and 80cm (31½ in) long. The knots are placed with a little space in between them, which makes it perfect for darker rope when placed against a light wall.

Knots used

Reverse lark's head knot (RLHK) page 21
Right-facing square knot (RFSK) page 18
Alternating square knot (ASK) page 19
Diagonal clove hitch (DCH) page 22
Overhand knot (OK) page 18

Materials

84m (92 yd) of twined 2.5mm ($\frac{1}{8}$ in) cotton rope
60cm (23$\frac{5}{8}$ in) wooden dowel

Equipment

Brush

Preparation

Cut the following:
26 cords, each 3.2m (3$\frac{1}{2}$ yd) long

Fold each of the cords in half and attach to the
dowel using a reverse lark's head knot (RLHK).

instructions

Step 1

Tie a row of 13 right-facing square knots (RFSK) underneath the dowel. Tie a second row of 12 alternating knots (ASK), skipping the first 2 and last 2 cords. Tie a third row of alternating square knots, skipping 4 cords between each knot

Step 2

Tie 5 rows of the fishbone pattern, with 4 right-facing square knots in each sennit. Note that in the first, middle and last sennit on the first row, the sennits begin just underneath the square knots from the previous step. For more detailed instructions for the fishbone pattern, see page 31.

Step 3

Use the filler cords from the sennits in the fourth row of the fishbone pattern as filler cords to tie 8 lines of diagonal clove hitches (DCH) in a zigzag pattern. Each diagonal should include 5 clove hitches.

Step 4

Tie a row of 7 alternating square knots, skipping 4 cords between each. Tie a second row of 12 alternating square knots and place them with about 1cm ($^3/_8$ in) of free cord from the knots above. Tie a third row of 13 alternating square knots.

Step 5

Begin the bottom part of the wall hanging with 6 rows of overlapping diamonds. Use cords 15, 16, 17 and 18 to tie an alternating square knot. Tie another using cords 35, 36, 37, 38. Finish the 2 first diamonds, each with 9 alternating square knots placed 1cm ($^3/_8$ in) apart.

Step 6

To continue with the second row of 3 diamonds, place the top square knots just slightly below the level of the middle of the previous diamonds. Finish the 3 diamonds, then continue with the third, fourth and fifth rows of 2 and 3 diamonds. The last row is only 1 diamond in the middle.

Step 7

Use cords 1–5 to tie an overhand knot (OK) around cords 6–10. Use cords 11–15 to tie an overhand knot around cords 16–20. Use cords 21 26 to tie an overhand knot around cords 27–32. Use cords 33–37 to tie an overhand knot around cords 38–42. Use cords 43–47 to tie an overhand knot around cords 48–52.

Step 8

Cut the ends, fray and then brush them for the finishing touch!

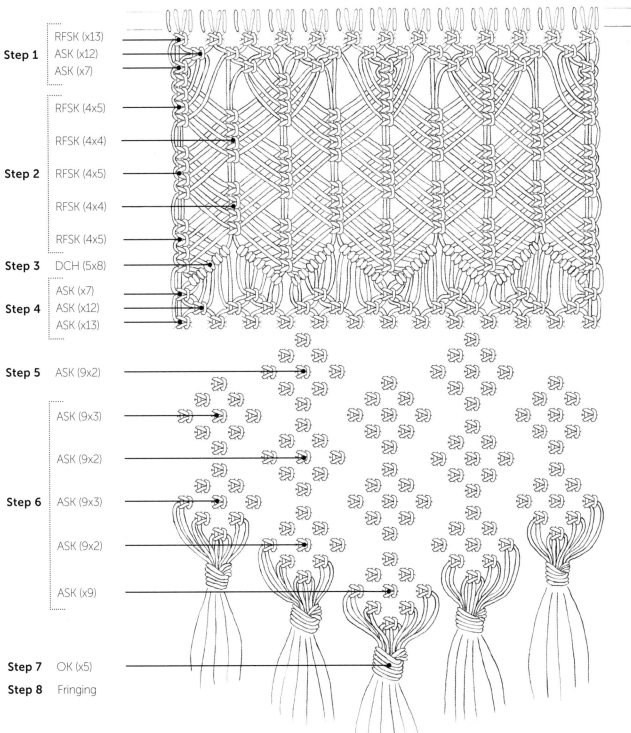

Start RLHK (x26)

Step 1
RFSK (x13)
ASK (x12)
ASK (x7)

Step 2
RFSK (4x5)
RFSK (4x4)
RFSK (4x5)
RFSK (4x4)
RFSK (4x5)

Step 3 DCH (5x8)

Step 4
ASK (x7)
ASK (x12)
ASK (x13)

Step 5 ASK (9x2)

Step 6
ASK (9x3)
ASK (9x2)
ASK (9x3)
ASK (9x2)
ASK (x9)

Step 7 OK (x5)

Step 8 Fringing

vera
wall hanging

This wall hanging is 75cm (29½in) wide and 115cm (45¼in) high. Its clean and geometric pattern looks incredible in a modern home or in a bohemian interior.

Knots used
Reverse lark's head knot (RLHK) page 21
Horizontal clove hitch (HCH) page 22
Right-twisting half square knot (RTHSK) page 20
Left-twisting half square knot (LTHSK) page 20
Diagonal clove hitch (DCH) page 22
Alternating square knot (ASK) page 19

Materials
243m (265³/₄ yd) of twined 4mm (³/₁₆ in) cotton rope
100cm (39³/₈ in), wooden dowel

Preparation
Cut the following:
1 cord, 7.2m (7⁷/₈ yd) long (extra-long to use
as filler cord for the horizontal clove hitches)
47 cords, each 5m (5¹/₂ yd) long

The cord numbering is always from 1 on the left
to 96 on the right, and refers to the cord position
at the start of the step.

instructions

Step 1
Fold the extra-long cord with 470cm (185 in) on the left side and 250cm (98½ in) on the right, and attach it near the left end of the dowel using a reverse lark's head knot (RLHK). Fold each of the remaining cords in half and attach to the dowel using a reverse lark's head knot, positioning them all to the right of the extra-long cord.

Step 2
Using the extra-long cord end as the filler cord, tie a row of horizontal clove hitches (HCH) working from left to right.

Step 3
Tie a row of 24 right-twisting half square knots (RTHSK), with 4 half square knots in each twist. Make sure that your extra long cord ends up at the far right.

Step 4
Alternate the filler cords and the working cords, and tie a row of 23 left-twisting half square knots (LTHSK), with 4 half square knots in each twist.

Step 5
Again using the extra-long cord end as the filler cord, tie a row of horizontal clove hitches, working from right to left. Place it directly underneath the left-twisting half square knots.

Step 6
Start with the first X-shape by using cord 2 as the filler cord to work one row of 22 diagonal clove hitches (DCH) from left to right, followed by 23 diagonal clove hitches from right to left using cord 48 as filler cord. The diagonals should point to each other and align at their ends. To connect them, tie one diagonal clove hitch using cord 2 as the filler cord and cord 48 as the working cord. Start the second X-shape by repeating this sequence using cord 49 from left to right and cord 95 from right to left.

Step 7
Tie another diagonal under each diagonal you completed in the previous step. For the first X-shape, use cord 1 as the filler cord to tie 20 diagonal clove hitches from left to right. Use cord 49 (previously used in the diagonal of the second X-shape) as the filler cord to tie 21 diagonal clove hitches from right to left.

For the second X-shape, take the cord previously used to tie the first clove hitch in the diagonal you just made, and tie a row of 20 diagonal clove hitches from left to right. Finally, use cord 96 (the cord at the far right) as the filler cord to tie a row of 20 diagonal clove hitches from right to left.

Step 8
Using cords 43-54, tie 8 alternating square knots (ASK) to form a small diamond, with the top square knot placed about 5–6cm (2–2⅜ in) from the diagonal clove hitches above.

Step 9
Finish the diagonals using the same filler cords as in step 6. Note that the second row of clove hitches in each X-shape bends and changes direction.

Step 10
Using the extra-long cord end now placed to the left as the filler cord, tie a row of horizontal clove hitches from left to right.

Step 11
Skip the first 2 cords and tie a row of 23 left-twisting half square knots, with 4 half square knots in each twist.

Step 12
Alternate the filler cords and working cords and tie a row of 24 right-twisting half square knots, with 4 half square knots in each twist.

Step 13
Use the extra long cord end as the filler cord to tie a row of horizontal clove hitches from right to left.

Step 14
Tie a row of 7 small diamonds just like the one you made in step 8, using alternating square knots and skipping 2 cords between each diamond. Continue the pattern by tying 3 more rows of diamonds underneath, with each row offset on the one above.

Step 15
Cut all the cords to the same length. Finish the wall hanging by fraying the last 35cm (14in) of each end.

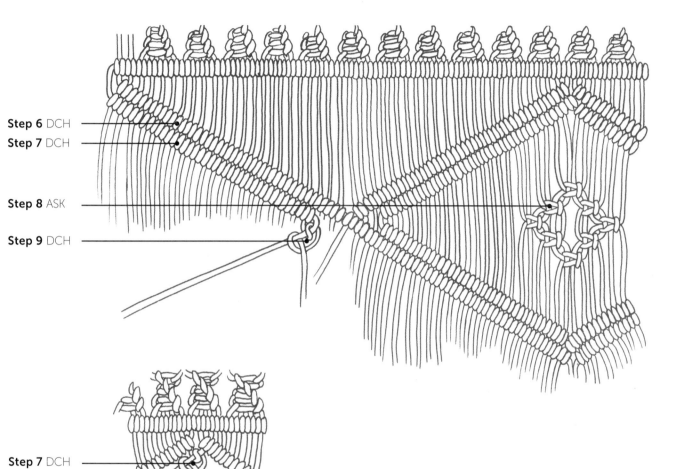

Step 6 DCH

Step 7 DCH

Step 8 ASK

Step 9 DCH

Step 7 DCH

Tip

To make the section with 2 large
X-shapes of diagonal clove hitches, you
will need to pay attention to the tilt of
your diagonals. If they tilt too much the
X-shapes will not reach the point where
they should cross, if you find this part
difficult, try to tilt them less than what
is shown in the illustration. You can also
test your angles by forming the X-shapes
with the filler cords. If anything needs
readjusting when you are done, try
moving the knots around on the filler
cord to force them into the right place.

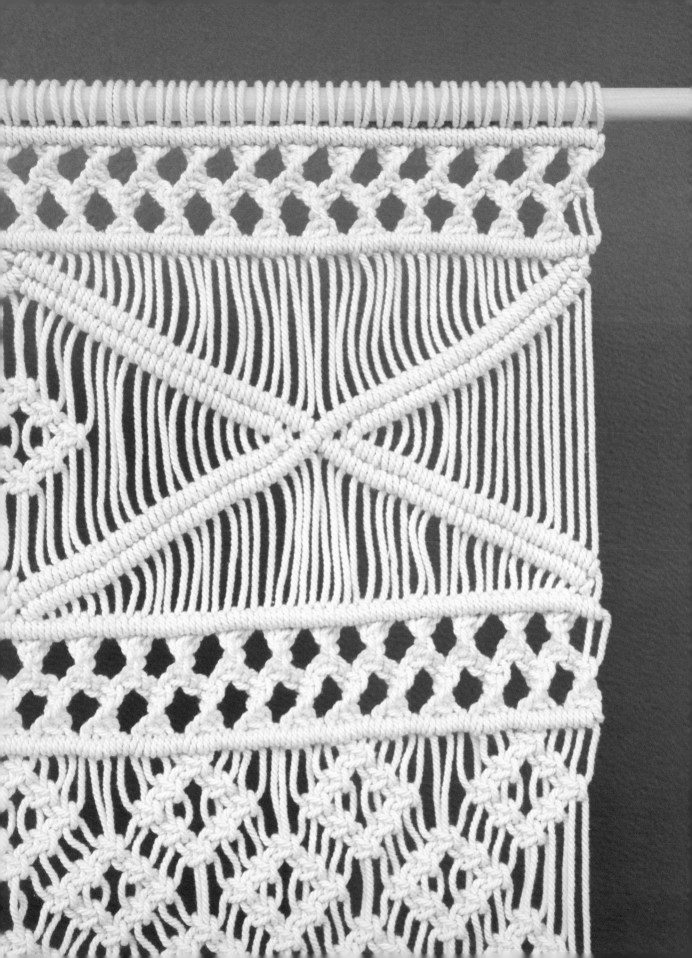

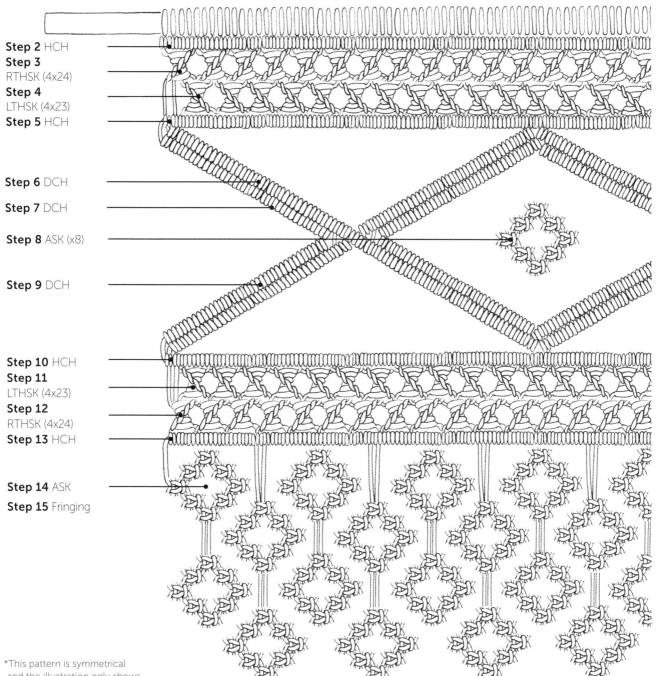

Step 1 RLHK (x48)

Step 2 HCH
Step 3
RTHSK (4x24)
Step 4
LTHSK (4x23)
Step 5 HCH

Step 6 DCH

Step 7 DCH

Step 8 ASK (x8)

Step 9 DCH

Step 10 HCH
Step 11
LTHSK (4x23)
Step 12
RTHSK (4x24)
Step 13 HCH

Step 14 ASK

Step 15 Fringing

*This pattern is symmetrical
 and the illustration only shows
 part of the design.

medusa
wall hanging

This gorgeous wall hanging is 105cm (41 $^3/_8$ in) wide and 120cm (47 $^1/_4$ in) high. It's made with over a thousand knots and will therefore take some time to finish, but the technique isn't complicated once you've mastered the square knot and clove hitch.

Knots used
Reverse lark's head knot (RLHK) page 21
Right-facing square knot (RFSK) page 18
Alternating square knot (ASK) page 19
Diagonal clove hitch (DCH) page 22

Materials
290m (317$^1/_8$ yd) of braided 5mm ($^1/_4$ in) cotton rope
130cm (51$^1/_4$ in) branch or dowel

Preparation
Cut the following:
12 cords, each 6m (6$^5/_8$ yd) long
24 cords, each 5.8m (6$^3/_8$ yd) long
14 cords, each 5.6m (6$^1/_8$ yd) long

The cord numbering is always from 1 on the left
to 100 on the right, and refers to the cord position
at the start of the step.

instructions

Step 1

Fold each 6m (6⅝yd) cord in half and attach to the middle of the branch or dowel, using a reverse lark's head knot (RLHK). Fold each 5.8m (6⅜in) cord in half and attach using a reverse lark's head knot, with 12 to the left of the middle cords and 12 to the right. Finally, fold each of the remaining 5.6m (6⅛in) cords in half and attach using a reverse lark's head knot, with 7 on each side of the cords already in place.

Step 2

Begin by skipping 2 cords and then tying a row of 24 right-facing square knots (RFSK), leaving 2 loose cords at the end.

For the second row, work 3 alternating square knots (ASK), skip 4 cords and work another 5 alternating square knots, skip 4 cords, work 5 more alternating square knots. Repeat this sequence until the second row is completed, ending with 3 alternating square knots.

For the third row, skip 2 cords and work 2 alternating square knots, skip 8 cords, work another 4 alternating square knots, skip 8 cords, work another 4 alternating square knots. Repeat this sequence until the third row is completed, ending with 2 alternating square knots and 2 loose ends.

For the fourth row, work 2 alternating square knots, skip 12 cords, work another 3 alternating square knots, skip 12 cords, work another 3 alternating square knots. Repeat this sequence until the forth row is completed, ending with 2 alternating square knots.

For the fifth row, skip 2 cords and work 1 alternating square knot, skip 16 cords, work 2 alternating square knots, skip 16 cords, work another 2 alternating square knots. Repeat this sequence until the fifth row is completed, ending with 1 alternating square knot and 2 loose ends.

For the sixth row, work 1 alternating square knot, skip 20 cords, work 1 alternating square knot, skip 20 cords. Repeat this sequence until the sixth row is completed, ending with 1 alternating square knot.

Step 3

To begin tying the four large diamonds in the pattern, use cord 15 as filler cord and tie 14 diagonal clove hitches (DCH) from right to left, placed with a little space under the square knots. Using cords 39, 63 and 87 as filler cords, tie diagonal clove hitches (12 clove hitches for each diagonal) from right to left for the other 3 diamonds. Continue the diagonal clove hitches from left to right, using the first working cords in the previous diagonals as filler cords, and stop when you meet the diagonal in the other direction, tying the two diagonals together.

For the last diagonal on the far right, continue tying all the way to the edge (13 diagonal clove hitches in total).

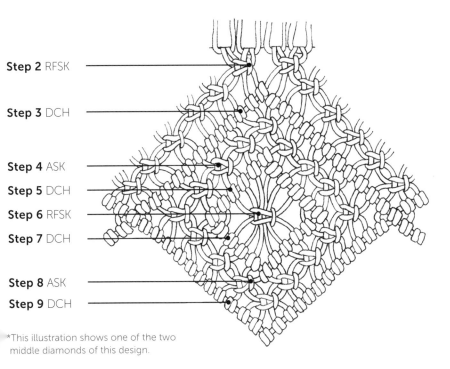

Step 2 RFSK

Step 3 DCH

Step 4 ASK
Step 5 DCH
Step 6 RFSK
Step 7 DCH

Step 8 ASK
Step 9 DCH

*This illustration shows one of the two
middle diamonds of this design.

<u>Step 4</u>
Tie the top 7 alternating square knots in
each diamond, placing them in a diagonal
line below the clove hitches but leaving
a little space.

<u>Step 5</u>
Make the top part of the inner diamond
with 6 diagonal clove hitches from right
to the left using cord 15 as the filler
cord. Then make 5 diagonal clove hitches
going from left to the right, using the
working cord for the first clove hitch
in the previous diagonal as filler cord.

<u>Step 6</u>
Tie a right-facing square knot in the
middle of each diamond, using four filler
cords in each.

<u>Step 7</u>
Using the last working cords as filler
cords, close the inner diamond by tying
4 diagonal clove hitches from left to right
and 5 diagonal clove hitches from right
to left.

<u>Step 8</u>
Tie the remaining 9 alternating square
knots for the bottom half of each
diamond.

<u>Step 9</u>
Finish the large diamonds by tying
diagonal clove hitches under the square
knots. Note that the diamonds on the
far left and right start their outer, bottom
diagonal after skipping 2 cords.

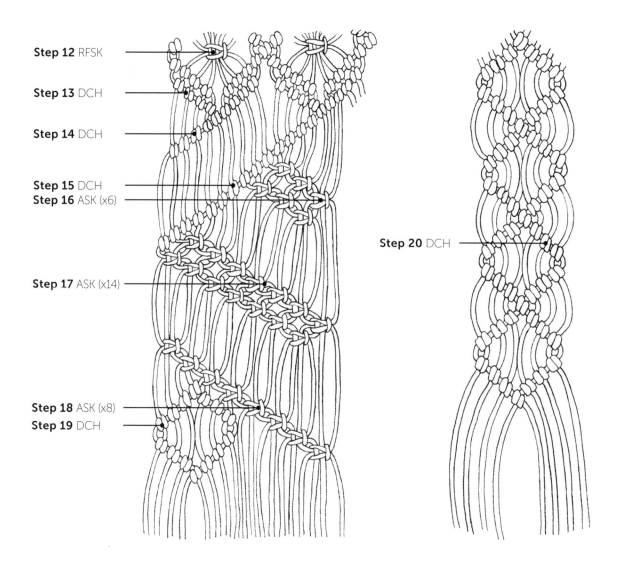

Step 12 RFSK

Step 13 DCH

Step 14 DCH

Step 15 DCH
Step 16 ASK (x6)

Step 17 ASK (x14)

Step 18 ASK (x8)
Step 19 DCH

Step 20 DCH

Step 10

Tie the 6 bottom rows of alternating square knots to finish the first part of the pattern, working step 2 in reverse.

Step 11

To begin the row of 10 diamonds right across the wall hanging, tie the first row of diagonal clove hitches. Start with cord 5 as the filler cord and tie 4 diagonal clove hitches from right to left, then use cord 6 as the filler cord to tie 4 diagonal clove hitches from left to right. Continue in this way to begin the other 9 diamonds, using cords 15 and 16, 25 and 26, 35 and 36, 45 and 46, 55 and 56, 65 and 66, 75 and 76, 85 and 86 and 95 and 96. For the second line of diagonal knots, begin with the left-to-right direction 4 diagonal clove hitches, and then continue the right-to-left direction 4 diagonal clove hitches, adding a fifth knot to tie the diagonals together.

Step 12

Tie a right-facing square knot in the middle of each diamond, each with 4 filler cords.

Step 13

Finish the diamonds by tying the 2 bottom rows of diagonal clove hitches, 4 diagonal clove hitches for every diagonal in each direction.

Step 14

On the left side, continue the right-to-left diagonal from the bottom of the first diamond. Tie 1 diagonal clove hitch to close the diamond, and then another 4 diagonal clove hitches to the edge. Mirror this sequence on the right side to continue the left-to-right diagonal from the bottom of the last (tenth) diamond.

Step 15

Repeat step 14 for the second and ninth diamonds, first tying 1 diagonal clove hitch to close them, and then another 14 diagonal clove hitches to the edges.

Step 16

Tie 3 alternating square knots on each side, using cords 11 to 18 on the left and cords 90 to 83 on the right. Tie another 3 alternating square knots underneath on each side, using cords 9 to 16 on the left and 92 to 85 on the right.

Step 17

Tie another 14 alternating square knots (2 rows with 7 in each) on both sides, using cords 1 to 18 on the left and cords 100 to 83 on the right.

Step 18

Drop 5cm (2in) and tie another row of alternating square knots, 8 on each side, using cords 1 to 18 on the left and cords 100 to 83 on the right.

Step 19

Tie a diamond using 8 cords underneath the last row of square knots. For the diamond to the left, begin with cord 5 as the filler cord and tie 4 diagonal clove hitches going right to left, then use cord 6 as the filler cord to tie 3 diagonal clove hitches from right to left. For the right diamond, begin with cord 96 as filler cord and tie 4 diagonal clove hitches going left to right, then use cord 95 as the filler cord to tie 3 diagonal clove hitches from left to right. Complete the bottom half of each diamond by tying 3 diagonal clove hitches from left to right and 4 diagonal clove hitches from right to left, using the last knot to tie the diagonals together.

Step 20

Tie a vertical link of 4 diamonds, using cords 19 to 26 on the left and cords 75 to 82 on the right, tying diagonal clove hitches as in step 19.

Step 21

Tie a vertical link of four slightly larger diamonds (see the illustration on the next page), using cords 27 to 36 on the left and cords 65 to 74 on the right, tying diagonal clove hitches as in step 19.

Step 22

Tie a vertical link of 5 diamonds, using cords 37 to 44 on the left and cords 57 to 64 on the right, tying diagonal clove hitches as in step 19.

Step 23

Use the remaining 12 cords in the middle (cords 45 to 56) to tie a vertical link of four large diamonds, tying diagonal clove hitches as in step 19.

Step 24

Finish the wall hanging by trimming the ends.

Step 1 RLHK (x50)

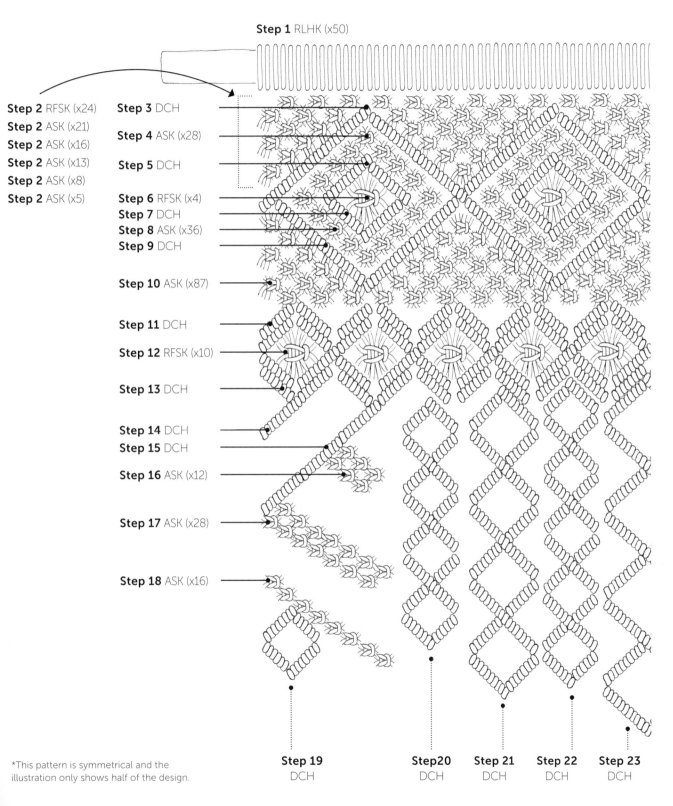

Step 2 RFSK (x24)
Step 2 ASK (x21)
Step 2 ASK (x16)
Step 2 ASK (x13)
Step 2 ASK (x8)
Step 2 ASK (x5)

Step 3 DCH

Step 4 ASK (x28)

Step 5 DCH

Step 6 RFSK (x4)
Step 7 DCH
Step 8 ASK (x36)
Step 9 DCH

Step 10 ASK (x87)

Step 11 DCH

Step 12 RFSK (x10)

Step 13 DCH

Step 14 DCH
Step 15 DCH

Step 16 ASK (x12)

Step 17 ASK (x28)

Step 18 ASK (x16)

*This pattern is symmetrical and the
illustration only shows half of the design.

Step 19
DCH

Step20
DCH

Step 21
DCH

Step 22
DCH

Step 23
DCH

eden
dream catcher

Making a tree pattern in a dream catcher is easier than you might think, and the result is stunning! The instructions will guide you to make a dream catcher 30cm (12 in) wide and 90cm (35½ in) long.

Knots used
Right-facing vertical lark's head knot (RFVLHK) page 21
Reverse lark's head knot (RLHK) page 21
Square knot (SK) page 18
Right-twisting half square knot (RTHSK) page 20
Alternating square knots (ASK) page 19
Horizontal clove hitch (HCH) page 22
Barrel knot (BK) page 25

Materials
43.7m (47 ¾ yd) of twined 2.5mm (⅛ in) cotton rope
Metal or wooden ring, 30cm (12 in) diameter

Preparation
Cut the following:
1 cord, 7.7m (8 ½ yd) long
10 cords, each 3.6m (4 yd) long

instructions

Step 1

Use the long 7.7m (8 ½ yd) cord to work right-facing vertical lark's head knots (RFVLH) around the ring, leaving about 25cm (10 in) of cord before the first knot. You can force the knots closer together to cover the ring better. When the ring is completely covered, take the loose ends and make the loop from which the dream catcher will hang.

Step 2

Fold the 10 remaining cords in half and attach each one to the ring using a reverse lark's head knot (RLHK), spacing them about 3–4cm (1⅛–1½ in) apart around the top of the ring, as shown in the illustration.

Step 3

Tie 5 adjacent square knots (SK) about 2cm (¾ in) away from the ring, then 4 alternating square knots (ASK) spaced underneath these, followed by 3 more alternating square knots.

Step 4

Take the 2 cords on each end and use them to tie a reverse lark's head knot to the ring on each side.

Step 5

Use the same cords and pair them with the 2 adjacent cords on both sides to tie a final alternating square knot on each side. Then using the 2 cords on each side, tie a 10–12cm (4–4¾ in) spiral of right-twisting half square knots (RTHSK) with all the other cords as the filler cords.

Step 6

To tie the cords to the bottom of the ring, begin with the middle cords and attach them using horizontal clove hitches (HCH). Then continue with the rest of the cords, placing each clove hitch as close together as possible. Make sure the cords are stretched and the clove hitches are tightened.

Step 7

Underneath the ring, tie 5 spirals of right-twisting half square knots. First use the 4 cords in the middle to tie a spiral with 5 turns. Then use the 3 cords on each side of the middle spiral to tie 2 more spirals, each with 6 turns. These spirals only have 1 filler cord. Use the next 3 cords on each side to tie 2 more spirals, each with 4 turns and only 1 filler cord in each. Leave the 2 remaining cords on each side as they are.

Step 8

Cut the cord ends so they are the same length and then tie a barrel knot (BK) on each cord, about 10cm (4 in) above the end.

Tip

To make a perfect rounded bottom edge to the fringe, hold the ring upside down, with the ends hanging freely, then cut them all in a straight line. When you turn the dream catcher upright, the ends will be shaped into a curve!

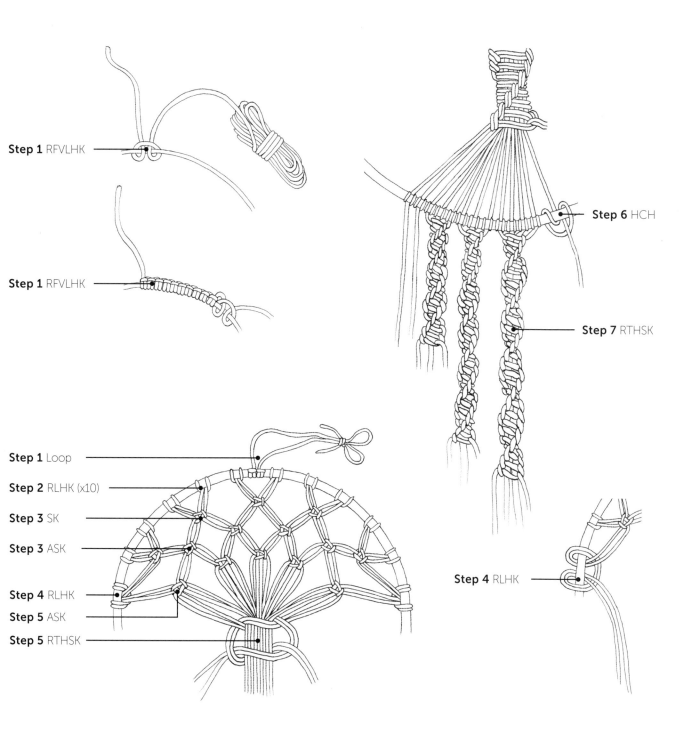

Step 1 RFVLHK

Step 1 RFVLHK

Step 1 Loop

Step 2 RLHK (x10)

Step 3 SK

Step 3 ASK

Step 4 RLHK

Step 5 ASK

Step 5 RTHSK

Step 6 HCH

Step 7 RTHSK

Step 4 RLHK

aurora
dream catcher

This little dream catcher does not take long to make but still looks really pretty! The instructions will guide you to make a dream catcher that is 22cm (8³/₄ in) wide and 85cm (33¹/₂ in) long.

Knots used
Right-facing vertical lark's head knot (RFVLHK) page 21
Reverse lark's head knot (RLHK) page 21
Horizontal clove hitch (HCH) page 22
Diagonal clove hitch (DCH) page 22
Alternating square knots (ASK) page 19
Square knot (SK) page 18

Materials
70m (76¹/₂ yd) of twined 2.5mm (¹/₈ in) cotton rope
Metal or wooden ring, 20cm (8 in) diameter

Preparation
Cut the following:
1 cord, 5.4m (6 yd) long (or 8 times
the circumference of the ring)
20 cords, each 3.2m (3¹/₂ yd) long

instructions

Step 1
Use the long 5.4m (6 yd) cord to work right-facing vertical lark's head knots (RFVLHK) around the ring, leaving about 25cm (10 in) of cord before the first knot. You can force the knots closer together to cover the ring better. When the ring is completely covered, take the loose ends and make the loop from which the dream catcher will hang. See the illustration for Step 1 on page 99.

Step 2
Take the 20 remaining cords, fold in half and attach them close together around the top of the ring using reverse lark's head knots (RLHK).

Step 3
Take the 2 middle cords and use each as a filler cord to work horizontal clove hitches (HCH) from the centre to the edges, a total of 19 clove hitches on each side.

Step 4
Use the third cord from the middle on each side as a filler cord to work a new row of horizontal clove hitches, a total of 16 clove hitches on each side. Place the knots directly under the previous row.

Step 5
Work 2 more rows on both sides, using the third cord from the beginning of the previous row as the filler cord each time.

Step 6
Now begin the top of the large diamond. Take the right middle cord as the filler cord to work 20 diagonal clove hitches (DCH) in a straight diagonal line from the centre to the left side, placing the knots underneath the 4 previous rows of clove hitches. Take the left middle cord (the cord used as working cord for the first clove hitch in the previous line), and use it as the filler cord to work 19 clove hitches in a straight line from the centre to the right.

Step 7
Tie a line of alternating square knots (ASK) underneath the diagonal clove hitches, 1 at the top and 8 on each side, so a total of 17 square knots

Step 8
To make the top of the little inner diamond, tie another 7 more alternating square knots in the middle, placed about 2–3cm ($^3/_4$–$1^1/_8$ in) from the previous line.

Step 9
Use the 2 middle cords as filler cords to work an upside down V-shape of diagonal clove hitches underneath the 7 square knots.

Step 10
Tie 1 square knot (SK), using the 4 cords in the middle.

Step 11
Close the little inner diamond, by first tying 2 lines of diagonal clove hitches underneath the middle square knot, and then tying 5 more alternating square knots under the clove hitches.

Step 12
Finish the larger diamond by tying alternating square knots placed about 2–3cm ($^3/_4$–$1^1/_8$ in) from the inner diamond, 7 on each side and one in the middle, a total of 15 alternating square knots. Take the cord furthest to the right and use it as the filler cord to work 19 diagonal clove hitches in a line from right to left, placed directly underneath the square knots. Finally, take the cord to the very left and use it as filler cord to work 20 diagonal clove hitches in a line from left to right, placed directly underneath the square knots.

Step 13
Attach the middle cords to the bottom of the ring using horizontal clove hitches, using the ring as the 'filler cord'. Continue with the rest of the cords, placing the clove hitches as close together as possible. Make sure the cords are stretched and the clove hitches tightened.

Step 14
Using the 4 middle cords, tie a square knot immediately under the ring. Then take the very left and right cords and use them as filler cords to work a row of diagonal clove hitches from each side towards the middle. Tie another square knot using the 4 middle cords.

Step 15
Finish the dream catcher by cutting the ends of the cords to make a fringe.

Tip
To make a perfect rounded bottom, hold the ring upside down, with the ends hanging freely, then cut them all in a straight line. When you turn the dream catcher upright, the ends will be shaped into a curve.

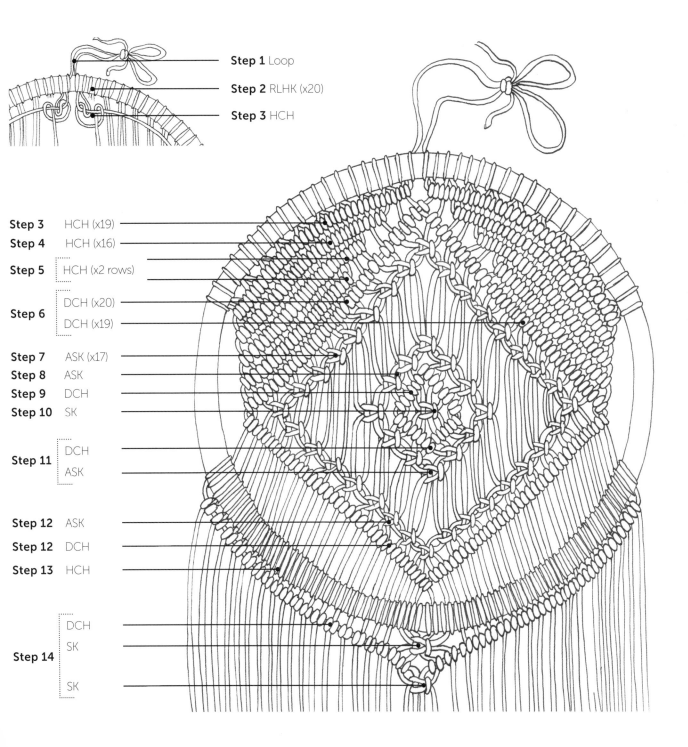

Step 1 Loop

Step 2 RLHK (x20)

Step 3 HCH

Step 3 HCH (x19)

Step 4 HCH (x16)

Step 5 HCH (x2 rows)

Step 6 DCH (x20)

DCH (x19)

Step 7 ASK (x17)

Step 8 ASK

Step 9 DCH

Step 10 SK

Step 11 DCH

ASK

Step 12 ASK

Step 12 DCH

Step 13 HCH

Step 14 DCH

SK

SK

leia
dream catcher

T-shirt yarn is perfect for making dream catchers, and it's a good way of experimenting with colours! The stretchy fabric makes it easy to achieve a perfect net in the ring. These instructions will guide you to make a 40cm (15³/₄ in) wide and 85cm (33¹/₂ in) long dream catcher.

Knots used
Square knot (SK) page 18
Square knot sennit (SK Sennit) page 18
Lark's head knot (LHK) page 20
Alternating square knots (ASK) page 19
4-ply crown knot (4-CK) page 25

Materials
Metal or wooden ring, 40cm (15³/₄ in) in diameter
25m (27³/₈ yd) of blue T-shirt yarn
20m (22 yd) of yellow T-shirt yarn
36m (39³/₈ yd) of pink T-shirt yarn

Preparation
Cut the following:
1 blue cord, 15m (16³/₈ yd) long
8 yellow cords, each 240cm (94¹/₂ in) long
4 pink cords, each 180cm (70⁷/₈ in) long
28 pink cords, each 100cm (39³/₈ in) long
24 blue cords, each 40cm (15³/₄ in) long,
used to make the blue tassels

instructions

Step 1

Fold the long 15m (16³/₈ yd) blue cord in half over the ring and work a sennit of square knots (SK) around the ring, using the ring as the 'filler cord'. You can force the knots closer together to make the ring show less between the knots. When the ring is completely covered, take the loose ends and make the hanging loop by tying a bow from which the dream catcher will hang.

Step 2

Fold the 8 yellow cords in half and attach each to the inner strand of a square knot on the ring, using a lark's head knot (LHK). Use a crochet hook if the square knots on the ring are too tight to push the cord through. Place 4 on each side of the hanging loop you created in step 1, each spaced about 4cm (1¹/₂ in) apart.

Step 3

Take the 4 long pink cords and attach them adjacent to the yellow cords using lark's head knots as in step 2, again spacing them 4cm (1¹/₂ in) apart.

Step 4

Begin the net for the dream catcher by tying 6 square knots about 3cm (1¹/₈ in) from the inner edge of the ring, 4 in yellow, and 2 in pink. Then tie 5 alternating square knots (ASK) underneath, 3 in yellow with 1 in yellow and pink on each side. Then make 4 more rows of alternating square knots with the yellow cords, with 4 in the first row, 3 in the second row, 2 in the third row and 1 in the last row.

Step 5

To continue the net, make sure you follow the illustration and use the right cords to tie the rest of the knots inside the ring. Attach the 2 yellow cords on the very left and right to the blue cord on the ring, by stretching them out using a crochet hook and knotting in place. This knot will later be covered by the blue tassels, so you don't have to make it a pretty knot, just make sure the cords are stretched.

Step 6

For the 3 pairs of yellow square knots at the bottom, place the working cords in front of the ring, and the filler cords behind, and tie 1 square knot for each underneath the ring to fasten the cords.

Step 7

Now take the pink cords and tie them together in front of the yellow cords using 4 alternating square knots placed slightly under the centre of the ring. Stretch 4 strands on each side out to the ring beside the yellow square knots, then attach them by using the outer cords as working cords to tie 1 square knot on each side underneath the ring.

Step 8

Take the 28 pink cords and fold each of them over the bottom of the ring, between the yellow square knots with 14 on each side of the centre yellow square knot. Tie 1 square knot with every 4 strands, with the cords folded behind the ring used as working cords. You'll have 7 square knots on each side.

Step 9

To make the blue tassels to go on each side, take 12 cords for each tassel, divide them in 2 and tie 2 rounds of a 4-ply crown knot (4-CK). Tighten the knot firmly and then take 2 cords and tie them around the ring, placing the tassels just on top of the knot you tied in step 5.

Step 10

Finish the dream catcher by cutting all the cords the length you would like.

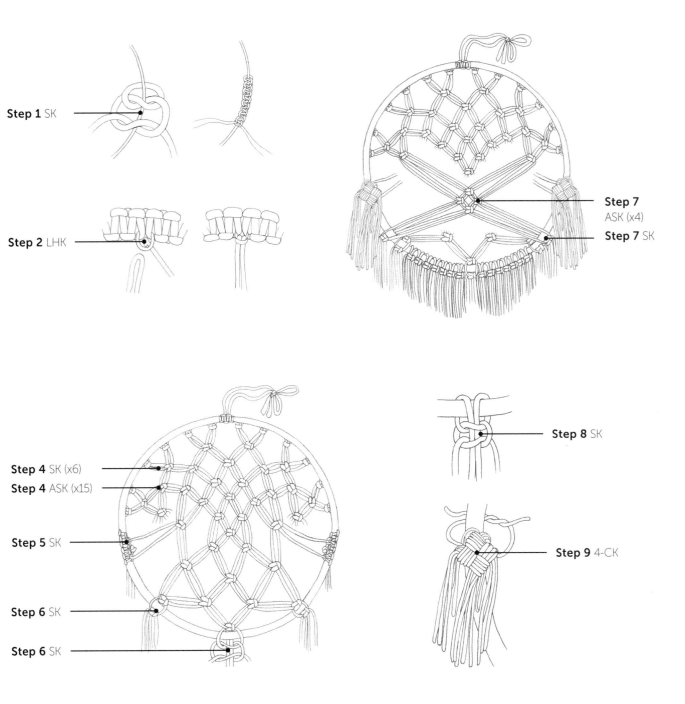

Step 1 SK

Step 2 LHK

Step 7 ASK (x4)

Step 7 SK

Step 4 SK (x6)

Step 4 ASK (x15)

Step 5 SK

Step 6 SK

Step 6 SK

Step 8 SK

Step 9 4-CK

place mat

Decorative macramé place mats can make any table setting look gorgeous. This design resonates with the design of the table runner on page 124, although the place mats are just as pretty on their own. Following these instructions will give you a place mat that measures 45 x 33cm (17³/₄ x 13 in).

Knots used

Horizontal clove hitch (HCH) page 22
Left-facing square knot (LFSK) page 18
Alternating square knot (ASK) page 19
Reverse lark's head knot (RLHK) page 21

Materials

60m (65⁵/₈ yd) of twined 2.5mm (¹/₈ in) cotton rope
55–60cm (21⁵/₈–23⁵/₈ in), dowel, at least 2cm (³/₄ in) in diameter (only used during the knotting)

Preparation

Cut the following:
20 cords, each 2m (2¹/₄ yd) long
4 cords, each 80cm (31¹/₂ in) long
52 cords, each 30cm (12 in) long
2 cords, each 50cm (19³/₄ in) long

Fold each of the 2m (2¹/₄ yd) cords in half and attach to the dowel, using a reverse lark's head knot (RLHK). Note: the dowel is only used during the knotting; it is removed at the end.

instructions

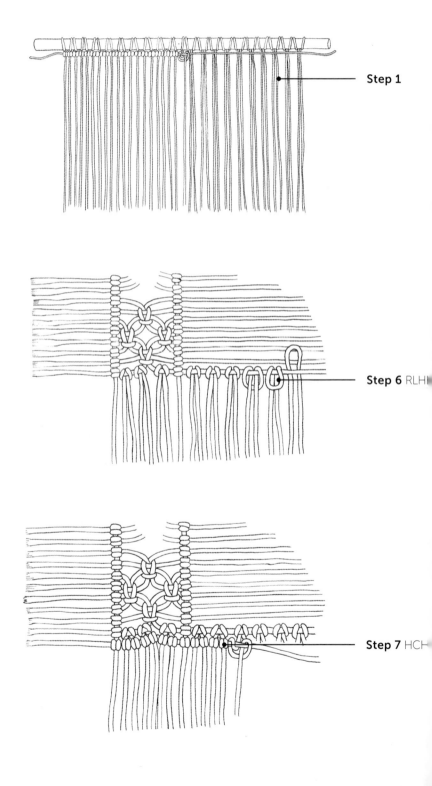

Step 1

Take 1 of the 80cm (31½ in) cords and lay it across so it's centered underneath the dowel. Using this cord as a filler cord, work a row of horizontal clove hitches (HCH) using each of the vertical cords, a total of 40 knots.

Step 1

Step 2

Skip 2 cords, tie a left-facing square knot (LFSK), skip 4 cords, tie another left-facing square knot, repeating to the end so you have 5 square knots. Tie 10 alternating square knots (ASK) for the second row. For the third row, skip 2 cords at the start and tie another 5 alternating square knots as in the first row.

Step 6 RLH

Step 3

Take a second 80cm (31½ in) cord and centre it beneath the knots just made. Using this cord as a filler cord, work a horizontal clove hitch with each of the vertical cords, a total of 40 knots.

Step 4

Tie a left-facing square knot using the 4 centre cords. Then work 2 alternating square knots underneath, then a line of 3 alternating square knots. Continue to create a pair of alternating square knots on each side to make the diamond in the centre of the mat as in the diagram, placing each pair of square knots just underneath the previous pair. Finish with a single left-facing square knot using the 4 centre cords. You'll have a total of 64 square knots.

Step 7 HCH

Step 5

Repeat steps 1–3 to create the border at the bottom of the mat. Turn the place mat 90 degrees.

Step 6

Attach 26 of the 30cm (12 in) long cords to what is now the bottom cord using reverse lark's head knots (RLHK). Position the first 3 lark's head knots between the 2 filler cord ends, then work 10 before the square knot of the centre diamond. Repeat in reverse with the rest of the cords on the other half of the mat.

Step 7

Take 1 of the 50cm (19³/₄ in) cords and lay it across so it's centred right underneath the lark's head knots. Using this cord as a filler cord, make a horizontal clove hitch with each cord from left to right, a total of 56 knots.

Step 8

Turn the place mat 180 degrees and repeat steps 6 and 7 for the other side.

Step 9

Remove the dowel and untangle the ends. Cut the loops to make a fringe, and then trim the ends on both short sides to the same length. Trim the remaining long side to the same length as the other side.

*This project is symmetrical and the illustration only shows half of the design.

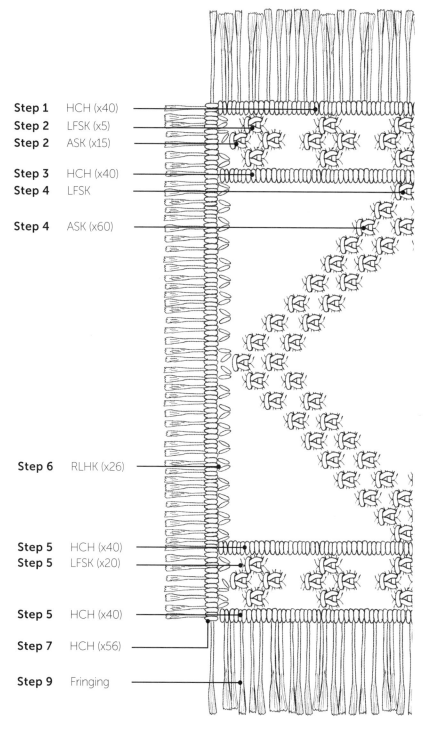

Step 1	HCH (x40)
Step 2	LFSK (x5)
Step 2	ASK (x15)
Step 3	HCH (x40)
Step 4	LFSK
Step 4	ASK (x60)
Step 6	RLHK (x26)
Step 5	HCH (x40)
Step 5	LFSK (x20)
Step 5	HCH (x40)
Step 7	HCH (x56)
Step 9	Fringing

lantern

A quite different, but very creative, project is to use macramé techniques to make a lantern to hang inside or outside. There are endless ways to do this, but these instructions will guide you to make a lantern 100cm (39³/₈ in) tall, and 30cm (12 in) in diameter. It is beautiful to hang just as it is, like a mobile, but the full effect is achieved if you can add light inside – although to avoid any fire risk, I would recommend using electric light. Safety first!

Knots used
Reverse lark's head knot (RLHK) page 21
Square knot (SK) page 18
Square knot sennit (SK Sennit) page 18
Alternating square knots (ASK) page 19
Horizontal clove hitches (HCH) page 22
Right-twisting half square knot (RTHSK) page 20
Barrel knot (BK) page 25

Materials
130m (142¹/₂ yd) of twined 2.5mm (¹/₈ in) cotton rope
1 metal ring, 30cm (12 in) in diameter
1 metal ring, 12cm (4³/₄ in) in diameter

Preparation
Cut the following:
19 cords, each 4m (4³/₈ yd) long
19 cords, each 2.8m (3¹/₈ yd) long

instructions

Step 1

Fold 1 of the longer cords in half and attach it to the smaller ring using a reverse lark's head knot (RLHK). Repeat with 1 of the shorter cords, and then continue to alternate long and short cords round the ring. Tie a round of right-facing square knots (SK) using the 2 strands of each short cord as filler cords and working with 1 strand of the longer cord on each side. Continue until you have tied all the cords to the ring.

Step 2

Tie a sennit of 4 more square knots after each square knot you tied in the previous step, making a total of 19 sennits with 5 square knots in each.

Step 3

Tie one round of alternating square knots (ASK), and then tie 1 square knot directly underneath each of these.

Step 4

Tie another round of alternating square knots, and then tie 4 square knots directly underneath each of these, to make another round of 5-knot sennits.

Step 5

For the next round of alternating square knots, increase the distance from the previous square knots just a little bit. Tie a second square knot directly underneath each square knot.

Step 6

Tie another round of alternating square knots, again spacing them a little from the previous round, as in step 5, and then tie 4 square knots in sennits directly underneath these.

Step 7

For the next round of alternating square knots, increase the distance from the previous square knots still further. Tie a second square knot directly underneath each square knot.

Step 8

Now attach the cords to the larger ring by tying one horizontal clove hitch (HCH) per cord, using the ring as the filler cord. Place the 19 sets of 4 cords at equal distance from each other on the ring.

Step 9

Tie a square knot underneath each set of 4 clove hitches to fasten securely the cords to the ring.

Step 10

Tie 3 laps of alternating square knots around the ring.

Step 11

Underneath the square knots, tie 5 half right-twisting square knots (RTHSK) to make small spirals around the lantern.

Step 12

You will notice that you have 2 different cord lengths. Tie 1 barrel knot (BK) on each of the short cords about 15cm (6in) above the end. Try to cut the short cords the same length as each other. Now tie 1 barrel knot on each of the longer cords at the same level as the ends of the shorter cords. Then cut the long cords the same length as each other – there should be about 15cm (6in) under the barrel knot. Fray the ends up to the barrel knots and you are done!

Tip

If you want to add a light to your lantern, the easiest way would be to hang a lightbulb inside the lantern from the same hook the lantern hangs off. To add a candle light, use wire to attach the top ring to fasten a candle light holder, but use caution when lighting the candle and do not leave it unattended.

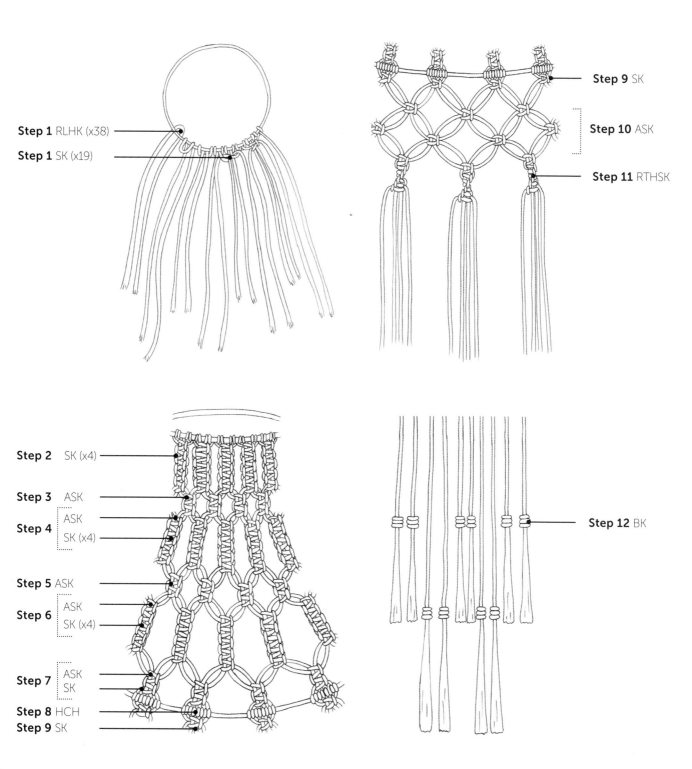

Step 1 RLHK (x38)

Step 1 SK (x19)

Step 9 SK

Step 10 ASK

Step 11 RTHSK

Step 2 SK (x4)

Step 3 ASK

Step 4 ASK / SK (x4)

Step 5 ASK

Step 6 ASK / SK (x4)

Step 7 ASK / SK

Step 8 HCH

Step 9 SK

Step 12 BK

garland

This decorative garland is 115cm (45¼ in) wide and 65cm (25⅝ in) high. The pattern is adjustable so that it can be repeated to make the garland longer, or you can use fewer repeats to make it shorter. The following instructions are for five repeats.

Knots used

Overhand knot (OK) page 18
Reverse lark's head knot (RLHK) page 21
Right-facing square knot (RFSK) page 18
Alternating square knot (ASK) page 19
Diagonal clove hitch (DCH) page 22
Wrap knot (WK) page 23

Materials
160m (175 yd) of twined or braided 4mm (³/₁₆ in) cotton rope

Preparation
Cut the following:
1 cord, 5m (5½ yd) long (horizontal anchor cord and hangers on the sides)
6 cords, each 3.6m (4 yd) long (for wrap knots)
74 cords, each 1.8m (2 yd) long

instructions

Step 1
To set up, fold the 5m (5½ yd) cord and tie an overhand knot (OK) so that the looped section is 150cm (60in) long. Hang the loop from 2 hooks, with the knot hanging in the middle, so that the loop is stretched out.

Step 2
Fold the 6 3.6m (4 yd) cords in half and attach each to the anchor cord (over both strands) using a reverse lark's head knot (RLHK), placing them 20–22cm (8–8¾ in) apart. The overhand knot will fall in the middle, between the third and fourth of the attached 3.6m (4 yd) cords.

Step 3
Fold 60 of the 1.8m (2 yd) cords in half and attach each to the anchor cord (over both strands) using a reverse lark's head knot, with 15 between each of the attached 3.6m (4 yd) cords, except between the middle third and fourth cords.

Step 4
Fold 12 of the 1.8m (2yd) cords in half and attach each to the anchor cord (over both strands) using a reverse lark's head knot, positioning them between the third and fourth attached 3.6m (4yd) cords so that 6 are to the left of the overhand knot, and 6 to the right. Untie the overhand knot on the anchor cord.

Step 5
Overlap the loose ends of the anchor cord and attach the 2 remaining 1.8m (2yd) cords over the overlapped section, (i.e. over 3 strands), using a reverse lark's head knot. The 2 ends of the anchor cord will be used as working cords.

Step 6
Skip the first cord, then begin the pattern with one row of right-facing square knots (RFSK), also skipping the last cord. When you reach the middle, use the ends of the anchor cords as filler cords in the square knots as normal.

Step 7
For the second row, skip the first 3 cords, then tie 3 alternating square knots (ASK), skip 4 cords, tie another 3 alternating square knots, skip 4 cords, repeating this sequence to the end and also skipping the last 3 cords. The ends of the anchor cord will be used as working cords in this row, which secures it.

Step 8
For the third row, skip the first 5 cords, tie 2 alternating square knots, skip 8 cords, tie 2 alternating square knots, skip 8 cords, repeating this sequence to the end and also skipping the last 5 cords.

Step 9
For the fourth row, tie 1 alternating square knot under each pair of square knots from the third row.

Step 10
Tie a right-facing square knot in the spaces between the pattern you have created, using 4 working cords and 4 filler cords. Place the knots level with the fourth row.

Step 11
Enclose the pattern under the large square knot using 7 alternating square knots to complete the point of each triangle shape, as shown in the illustration.

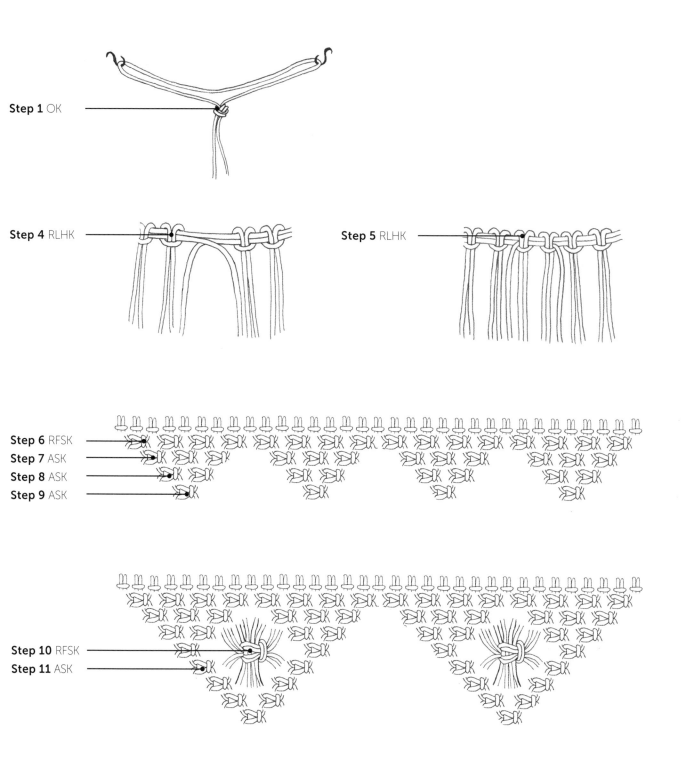

Step 1 OK

Step 4 RLHK

Step 5 RLHK

Step 6 RFSK
Step 7 ASK
Step 8 ASK
Step 9 ASK

Step 10 RFSK
Step 11 ASK

Step 12

Tie a line of diagonal clove hitches (DCH) underneath the pattern. Use the loose ends at the edges as filler cords for the first and last diagonal, and the working cords in the square knots at the edges of the triangles as filler cords for the remaining diagonals.

Step 13

Between each triangle, tie another 7 diagonal clove hitches on one side, and 6 on the other, placing them under the previous diagonal clove hitches.

Step 14

Tie 8 alternating square knots in the shape of a diamond, placing them underneath the diagonal clove hitches in the previous step.

Step 15

Enclose the diamond by tying diagonal clove hitches directly underneath the alternating square knots. Each diagonal going from left to right should include 5 clove hitches. Whereas each diagonal going right to left should include 6 clove hitches with the sixth tying the diagonals together.

Step 16

Continue the diagonal clove hitches down towards the tip of each triangle, but for each finished knot take the working cord and place it together with the filler cord, thus adding one more filler cord after each finished knot. This makes the diagonal clove hitches thicker and thicker as you go. Be sure to tighten the knots firmly.

Step 17

Gather the loose ends at the bottom of each triangle and use one of the long cords to tie a wrap knot (WK) under each triangle.

Step 18

Finish the garland by trimming the cords to the desired length.

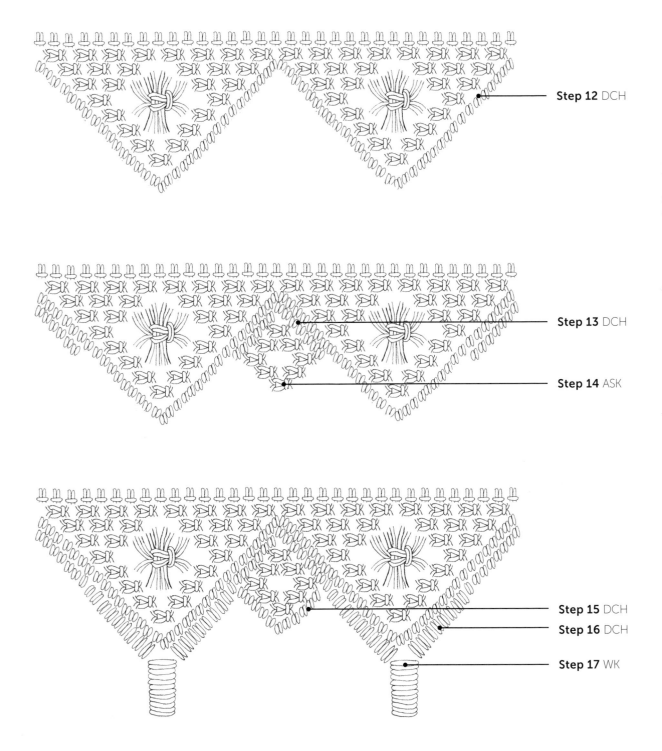

Step 12 DCH

Step 13 DCH

Step 14 ASK

Step 15 DCH

Step 16 DCH

Step 17 WK

tassels

Making tassels is an easy way to use up some of your short leftover rope. You can pass a string through the head of the tassel and create a garland out of several tassels, or hang them individually.

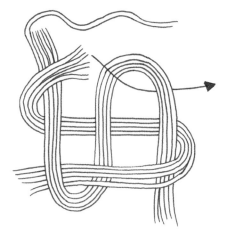

Knots used
4-ply crown knot (4-CK) page 25
Wrap knot (WK) page 23

Materials
Leftover rope

Equipment
Brush

Preparation
Cut the following:
7 short cords, each about twice the length of the desired finished tassel
1 cord, about 70cm (28in) long (this cord should always be longer than the rest as it is used to make the wrap knot).

instructions

Step 1 Take 4 short cords and lay them down vertically, then place the other 3 short cords and the long cord horizontally on top, to form a cross shape.

Step 2 Tie 3 rounds of the 4-ply crown knot (4-CK) using all the cords.

Step 3 Take the long cord and tie a wrap knot (WK) underneath the crown knot.

Step 4 Pull all the strands to tighten the wrap knot under the crown knot.

Step 5 Lose the long end among all the other tassel ends, trimming it to the same length if necessary. Fray your cord ends and brush them to get a fluffy, fuller effect.

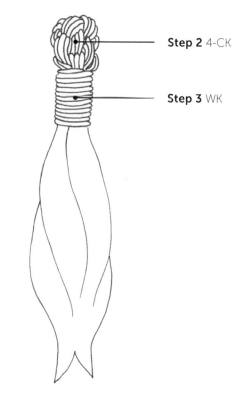

Step 2 4-CK

Step 3 WK

table
runner

A macramé table runner can seem an ambitious project, but the reward is worth it! The instructions will help you with the measurements to make a 2.5m ($2^3/_4$ yd) long and 25cm (10 in) wide table runner. The design uses a repeat pattern with two different sections; a large diamond and several small diamonds. The first section is repeated five times with the second pattern in between repeated four times.

Knots used

Overhand knot (OK) page 18
Reverse lark's head knot (RLHK) page 21
Horizontal clove hitch (HCH) page 22
Right-facing square knot (RFSK) page 18
Alternating square knot (ASK) page 19

Materials

204m (224yd) of twined 2.5mm ($^1/_8$ in) cotton rope
50–60cm ($19^3/_4$–$23^5/_8$ in) dowel (only used during the knotting)

Preparation

Cut the following:
20 cords, each 10m (11yd) long
10 cords, each 35cm (14in) long

Fold each of the 10m (11yd) cords in half and tie an overhand knot (OK) 25cm (10 in) below the fold. Attach each cord to the dowel using reverse lark's head knots (RLHK) with the ends hanging (these will later be the fringe). Note: the dowel is only used during the knotting; it is removed at the end. See the illustration on page 127.

instructions

Step 1

Take 1 of the 35cm (14 in) cords and tie an overhand knot at one end. Lay it across the vertical cords and below the dowel, with the overhand knot just to the left of the vertical cords. Using this cord as a filler cord, work a horizontal clove hitch (HCH) with each of the vertical cords, a total of 40 clove hitch knots. Tie another overhand knot after the last clove hitch. The overhand knots make sure that the filler cord doesn't slip out.

Step 2

To begin the first large diamond, tie a right-facing square knot (RFSK) using the 4 centre cords, placed just under the clove hitches. Then work 2 alternating square knots (ASK) underneath, then a line of 3 alternating square knots. Continue to create a pair of alternating square knots on each side to make the diamond in the centre as in the diagram, placing each pair of square knots just underneath the previous pair. Finish with a single right-facing square knot using the 4 centre cords. You'll have a total of 64 square knots.

Step 3

Repeat step 1 with another 35cm (14 in) cord as filler cord for another row of 40 horizontal clove hitches placed underneath the diamond.

Step 4

To begin the section with 4 rows of small diamonds, skip 2 cords, tie a right-facing square knot underneath the clove hitches, skip 4 cords, tie another right-facing square knot, repeating to the end so you have 5 square knots. Tie 10 alternating square knots for the second row directly beneath your first row. For the third row, skip 2 cords at the start and tie another 5 alternating square knots as in the first row.

Step 5

Drop 4cm (1½ in) before beginning the next row of diamonds. Skip 6 cords, tie a right-facing square knot, skip 4 cords, tie another right-facing square knot, repeating to the end so you have 4 square knots. Tie 10 alternating square knots for the second row. For the third row, skip 6 cords at the start and tie another 4 alternating square knots as in the first row.

Step 6

Repeat steps 4 and 5 to finish the section of small diamonds.

Step 7

Repeat step 1 with another 35cm (14 in) cord as filler cord for a row of 40 horizontal clove hitches placed underneath the last square knots.

Step 8

Continue by repeating steps 2–7 three times. Finish by repeating steps 2–3 for another large diamond.

Step 9

Remove the dowel and untie the overhand knots. Cut the loops to make a fringe, and then trim the cords on both ends to the same length. Cut the filler cords for the horizontal clove hitches to 1cm (³⁄₈ in) from the overhand knots.

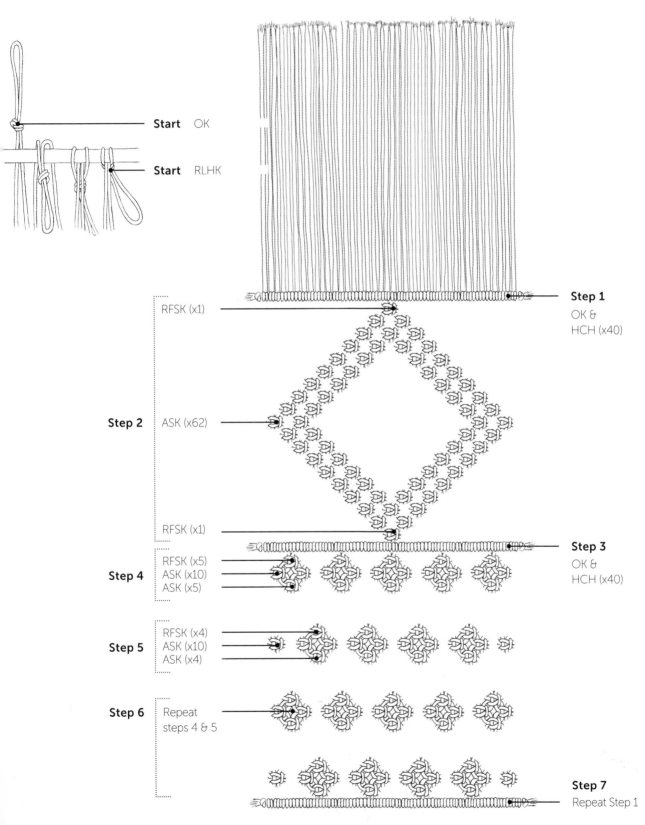

Start OK

Start RLHK

RFSK (x1) — **Step 1**
OK &
HCH (x40)

Step 2 | ASK (x62)

RFSK (x1) — **Step 3**
OK &
HCH (x40)

Step 4 | RFSK (x5)
ASK (x10)
ASK (x5)

Step 5 | RFSK (x4)
ASK (x10)
ASK (x4)

Step 6 | Repeat
steps 4 & 5

Step 7
Repeat Step 1

table runner **127**

curtain

A macramé curtain is beautiful in any doorway and is a perfect way to cover an open closet to draw attention away from what's inside. This pattern creates a 90cm (35½in) wide curtain, but since it uses a repeated pattern you can add or subtract cords to make it wider or narrower. Depending on how many barrel knots you tie, the length of the curtain will vary.

Knots used
Reverse lark's head knot (RLHK) page 21
Horizontal clove hitch (HCH) page 22
Right-facing square knot (RFSK) page 18
Alternating square knot (ASK) page 19
Diagonal clove hitch (DCH) page 22
Alternating half hitch (AHH) page 23
Right-twisting half square knot (RTHSK) page 20
Barrel knot (BK) page 25

Materials
481m (526¾yd) of twined or braided 4mm (³/₁₆in) cotton rope
120cm (47¼in) wooden bar, thick enough to carry the weight of your curtain

Preparation
Cut the following:
59 cords, each 8m (8¾yd) long
1 cord, 9m (9⅞yd) long

instructions

Step 1
Attach each of the shorter cords to the bar using a reverse lark's head knot (RLHK).

Step 2
Attach the longer cord to the left of the other cords, using a reverse lark's head knot and folded with 4m (4³/₈ yd) of cord to the right, and 5m (5¹/₂ yd) to the left.

Step 3
Tie a row of horizontal clove hitches (HCH) from left to right, using the extra-long cord as the filler cord.

Step 4
For the first row, skip 1 cord, tie 2 right-facing square knots (RFSK), skip 2 cords and tie 2 more right-facing square knots. Work across the first row by switching between tying 2 right-facing square knots and skipping 2 cords. For the second row, tie alternating square knots (ASK) by skipping 3 cords, tying 1 square knot, skipping 6 cords, tying 1 square knot. Work across the second row by switching between tying 1 square knot and skipping 6 cords.

Step 5
Using the cords you skipped on the first row as filler cords, tie a line of diagonal clove hitches (DCH) under the square knots. Each diagonal going from right to left should include 4 clove hitches. Each diagonal going from left to right should include 5 clove hitches, with the fifth tying the diagonals together.

Step 6
In each triangular space between the diagonals, tie a set of 4 alternating square knots to form smaller diamond shapes. At the very left and right of the panel, only tie 1 right-facing square knot using the 4 cords on each side.

Step 7
Using the set of 4 cords between each set of alternating square knots, tie a sennit of 3 right-facing square knots.

Step 8
Use the filler cords from the sennits in step 7 to tie diagonal clove hitches. Each diagonal going from right to left should include 4 clove hitches. Each diagonal going from left to right should include 5 clove hitches, with the fifth tying the diagonals together. You'll have 11 hexagonal shapes across the width.

Step 9
Repeat steps 6–8 once more to continue the pattern as shown in the diagram on page 132. Note that on this second repeat, there will only be 2 cords on each side, which are used to tie 4 alternating half hitches (AHH). You'll have 12 hexagonal shapes across the width.

Step 10
On the third repeat of steps 6–8, continue the pattern but on each of the centre 4 sets of cords in step 7 replace the sennit with a spiral of 3 turns using right-twisting half square knots (RTHSK). Complete 3 of the hexagon shapes on each side with step 8, but leave the remaining centre cords loose.

Step 11
On the fourth repeat of steps 6–8, tie 4 alternating half hitches with the 2 cords on each edge, then work the pattern as set to make 3 hexagons on each side. Skip 1 cord and tie a spiral with 3 turns using right-twisting half square knots on the next set of 4 cords, leaving the remaining centre cords loose.

Step 12
On the fifth repeat of steps 6–8 there will only be 1 complete hexagon on each side, with the second hexagon only worked to step 6 and the sennit replaced with a spiral with 2 turns using right-twisting half square knots. On the sixth repeat of steps 6–8 there will only be 2 cords on each side, which are used to tie 4 alternating half hitches. Tie 1 hexagon, then skip 1 cord and tie a spiral with 2 turns using right-twisting half square knots. Complete the design with a final spiral beneath the last hexagon, again with only 2 turns.

Step 13
When you have finished the upper part of the curtain the cords are still quite long. Tie several barrel knots (BK) at random points along each cord to shorten them and create the lower part of the pattern. Trim the ends to the length you want the curtain to be.

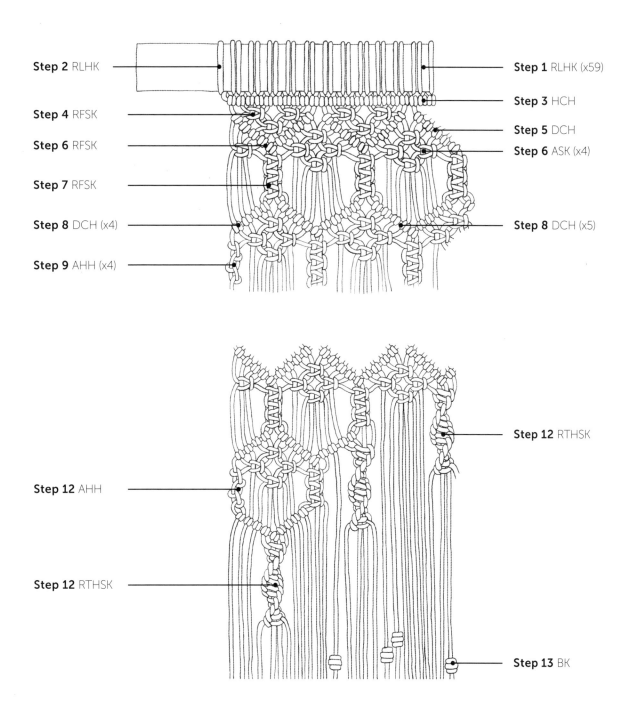

Step 2 RLHK

Step 1 RLHK (x59)

Step 3 HCH

Step 4 RFSK

Step 5 DCH

Step 6 RFSK

Step 6 ASK (x4)

Step 7 RFSK

Step 8 DCH (x4)

Step 8 DCH (x5)

Step 9 AHH (x4)

Step 12 RTHSK

Step 12 AHH

Step 12 RTHSK

Step 13 BK

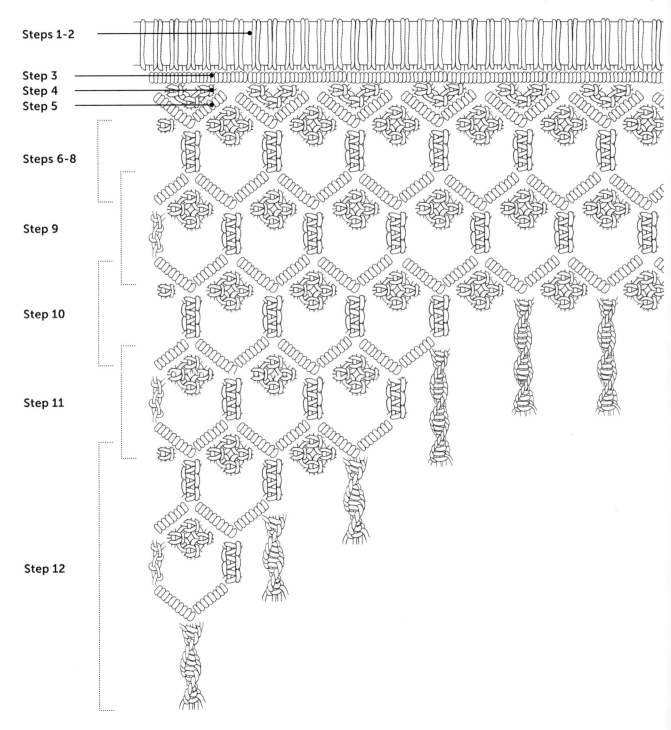

*This pattern is symmetrical and the illustration only shows half of the design.

Steps 1-2

Step 3
Step 4
Step 5

Steps 6-8

Step 9

Step 10

Step 11

Step 12

bench

Making a bench or a stool with macramé details is like a final test before completing your macramé training. It can be a bit time-consuming, but if you know your knots it shouldn't be too hard! In fact, the trickiest part can be to find the frame for the seat, which is why I built mine myself. If you do not want to build the frame, look for a bench or stool with fabric for the seat and then remove this. The instructions are to make a knotted seat about 80cm (31½ in) long and 44cm (17¼ in) deep, but you can choose to skip the butterfly pattern, add cords to make a longer bench, or use fewer cords to make a stool. The most important thing to remember is to use strong rope that won't stretch or break!

Knots used

Reverse lark's head knot (RLHK) page 21
Square knot (SK) page 18
Alternating square knot (ASK) page 19
Horizontal clove hitch (HCH) page 22
Lark's head knot (LHK) page 20

Materials

About 230m (252 yd), twined or braided 4mm (³/₁₆ in) strong cotton rope
Bench frame, about 80 x 40cm (31½ x 17¼ in)

Preparation

36 cords, each 5.4m (6 yd) long (used to make the seat and the long front side)
16 cords, each 2m (2¼ yd) long (used to make the sides of the two ends of the bench)

These were the cords used for this bench.

The number of cords you need is dependent on the size of the frame for your seat, so cut the cords one by one and lay them on the seat to see how many you need. Begin with the cords for the seat (the long cords) and cut the shorter cords for the sides after you have tied the seat.

The lengths of the cords, however, will not vary too much if you wish to make the butterfly pattern.

Prepare the frame for the bench or stool, for example by removing fabric or any other objects that will be in the way or are not needed. Since the knots need to be tied extra firmly, you might want to use pliers to avoid strain on your hands.

instructions

Step 1

To begin tying the seat of the bench, fold all your long cords in half and fasten them onto one of the long sides of the bench's frame, using reverse lark's head knots (RLHK). Leave a little space between each set of 4 cords, as shown in the illustration.

Step 2

Tie a row of square knots (SK), securing all the cords to the frame. Make sure that the knots are tied as tightly as possible, preferably using pliers.

Step 3

Tie a second row of alternating square knots (ASK) to begin the pattern for the seat. Begin with cords 3–6, skip 4 cords, tie another square knot then skip 4 cords, and continue following the illustration on page 139.

Step 4

When you have reached the other side of the frame, fasten the first cord using a horizontal clove hitch (HCH). Since you are using the frame as 'filler' for the knot, it is a little tricky. The most important thing is that the cord is stretched as tight as possible. Continue with the rest of the cords: skip 2 cords, tie 2 more clove hitches, skip 2 cords, tie 2 more clove hitches, and continue.

Step 5

To begin the front of the seat, tie a row of square knots just underneath the frame. Use the cords you tied the clove hitches with in the previous step as working cords for the knots, while the cords you skipped are used as filler cords coming from behind the frame.

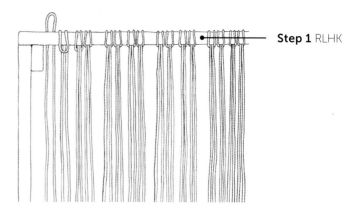

Step 1 RLHK

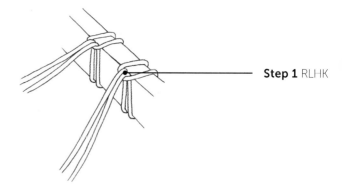

Step 1 RLHK

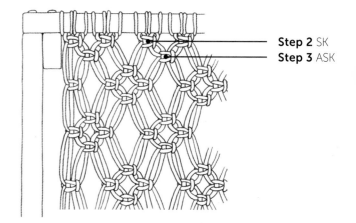

Step 2 SK
Step 3 ASK

Step 6

Tie 2 more rows of alternating square knots across the cords.

Step 7

Separate the cords into 4 sets. These sets will be used to make the 4 butterflies. See page 32 for detailed instructions on how to tie butterflies.

Step 8

Finish the front of the seat by tying 3 more rows of alternating square knots.

Step 9

To start the sides of the seat, fasten the short cords to the cords on the sides of the seat using lark's head knots (LHK) as seen on the illustration on page 139.

Step 10

Using the first cord, tie a horizontal clove hitch around the frame, as in step 4. Skip 2 cords, tie 2 more clove hitches, skip 2 cords, and continue.

Step 11

Tie a row of square knots just underneath the frame. Use the cords you tied the clove hitches with in the previous step as working cords for the knots, while the cords you skipped are used as filler cords coming from behind the frame.

Step 12

Tie a second row of alternating square knots. Begin with cords 3–6, skip 4 cords, tie another square knot then skip 4 cords, and continue according to the pattern as seen on the illustration on page 139.

Step 13

Finish your bench by cutting the cords the same length.

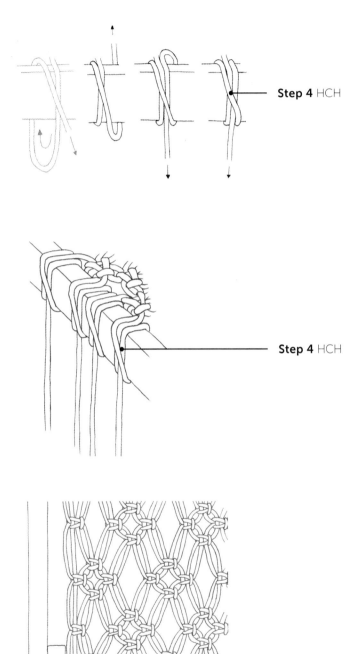

Step 4 HCH

Step 4 HCH

Step 4 HCH

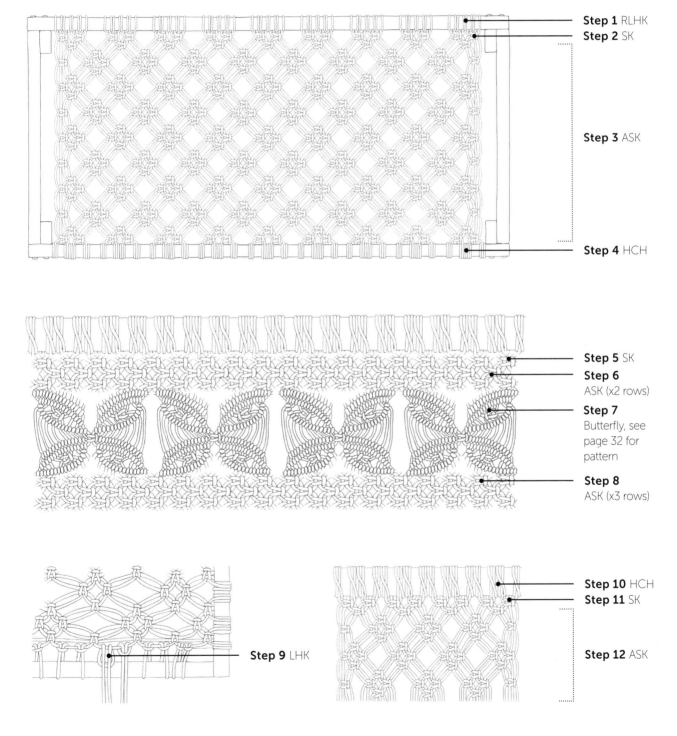

Step 1 RLHK

Step 2 SK

Step 3 ASK

Step 4 HCH

Step 5 SK

Step 6
ASK (x2 rows)

Step 7
Butterfly, see
page 32 for
pattern

Step 8
ASK (x3 rows)

Step 9 LHK

Step 10 HCH

Step 11 SK

Step 12 ASK

index

glossary

alternating

In macramé, alternating refers to the switching between filler cords and working cords for each tied row of knots. For example, when tying alternating square knots, your filler cords in the first row will be used as the working cords to tie the knots in the second row, while the working cords in the first row will become the filler cords in the second row.

anchor cord

Cord used instead of a dowel or branch, to which working cords are attached.

bar

The bar is a version of dowel, rod or pole, but refers to an item that is not rounded; rather it is flat with sharper edges.

body

The body is the main section of a project which is created as you knot. This is also known as a panel.

braid

A braid is made when three or more cords are intertwined in a pattern, rather than tied together using knots.

bundle (to bundle or a bundle)

When you group together a set of cords, either to separate and organize them while you are working, or as a decorative finishing touch on your cords' ends.

diagonal

In this book, a diagonal refers to a sequence of knots tied diagonally. They are tied either using diagonal clove hitches, or using alternating square knots.

dowel

Another word for rod or pole. In macramé, a dowel is used as support for your work to which the cords are attached. Dowels are most commonly used for wall hangings.

filler cord

A cord that runs through knots and is knotted around. The filler cord is not used for tying the knots.

fray

To separate the threads of your rope. Done in order to create a fluffy, decorative effect at the end of your piece of work.

fringe

A decorative border of cords or thread hanging loosely. In macramé, the fringe often refers to the bottom part of a project, when the cord ends are left long and loose.

hitch

A knot that is used to attach cords to other items.

linking cord

Cord that links together parts of your work. The linking cords are the cords that run between two knots spaced apart from each other, and can be both working cords and filler cords.

net

A net forms when you tie alternating knots (i.e. alternating your working cords and filler cords). For example, plant hangers have a net (often using square knots) in order for the plant to be held within the hanger.

panel

The panel is the main section of a project which is created as you knot. This is also known as a body.

picot

A small, decorative loop formed along the edge of a sennit.

row

In this book, a row refers to one sequence of tied knots where the knots are level horizontally, i.e. placed parallel to each other and not below each other or in a diagonal.

sennit

A series of the same knots tied subsequently. Alternatively: A sennit is formed when two or more of the same knots are tied subsequently. For example, if you tie five square knots in repeat, you have a sennit of five square knots. Or: A sennit is formed when a series of the same knots are tied subsequently.

strand

A generic term for cords, strings, rope and strips.

weave

When you pass a strand across other strands by threading it over and under in sequence.

working cord

The active cords used for tying the knots, as opposed to filler cords.

acknowledgments

This book would not have been possible had it not been for the amazing support of a number of people who have helped me in different ways.

Without a doubt, the one person who deserves the most thanking and has been the most crucial in making this book a reality is my partner and big love, Simon. Simon, thank you for your unbelievable selflessness and patience, for all the meals you cooked for me, for your comfort when I doubted myself, for your stubbornness to make me believe in my capabilities, and for pushing me to do and be better. Thank you for all the times you dropped everything to review texts, help me cut ropes, fray ends and even tie knots with me. You are incredible, I could not have done it without you.

I would also like to thank my wonderful parents who all my life believed in my crazy crafting endeavours more than I have myself, for investing time and money early in my life to let me follow my passion. Your constant support is and will always be invaluable.

This book would never have happened had it not been for Harriet at Quadrille Publishing who reached out to me and initiated it. Harriet, thank you for being an endless source of advice and for all your very hard work in helping me put this book together. Thank you for believing in my abilities and for helping me accomplish this dream.

There are so many more people to whom I owe gratitude for supporting me while working on this book. My friends who are always there for me with love and friendship, even when I completely disappeared to work on this book. My former boss, Petra, who put up with me at times of ecstatic outbursts and frustration, and always cheered me on. Anders, who took the time to provide me with indispensable advice and information during the initial phase of the book. Claire, Kim and Vanessa who have done amazing work to make this book look its very best. And Alice and her family, whose hospitality allowed me a quiet place to work from while I was travelling in Australia.

In this day and age, social media can have major and unexpected impacts in our lives. It is thanks to Instagram that I found macramé to begin with and could start sharing this passion with others. So thank you Instagram for being an endless source of inspiration for so many, for providing a platform for a community of creatives and inspiration seekers where it is possible to find love and support from all over the world.

Finally, I want to thank my followers on Instagram. You inspired me to keep exploring macramé, to open my shop, to start teaching macramé lessons and finally to write this book. Your love and support from day one when I started my account has been overwhelming and I am so thankful to all of you! This book is dedicated to you.

Publishing director: Sarah Lavelle
Editor: Harriet Butt
Creative director: Helen Lewis
Art direction: Claire Rochford
Designer: Vanessa Masci
Photographer: Kim Lightbody
Production director: Vincent Smith
Production controller: Tom Moore

First published in 2017 by Quadrille Publishing
Pentagon House, 52–54 Southwark Street,
London SE1 1UN
www.quadrille.com

Quadrille Publishing is an imprint of Hardie Grant
www.hardiegrant.com

Reprinted in 2017 (twice)
10 9 8 7 6 5 4 3

Cataloguing in Publication Data: a catalogue for this book
is available from the British Library.

ISBN 978 184949 940 8

31901060838929

Printed in China